MY FAMILY, MY CHURCH

My Family,
My Church

ROB & MARION WHITE

KINGSWAY PUBLICATIONS
EASTBOURNE

ISBN 0 86065 323 4

Unless otherwise indicated, biblical quotations are from
the New American Standard Bible, © The Lockman
Foundation
1960, 1962, 1963, 1968, 1971, 1972, 1973

RSV = Revised Standard Version
copyrighted 1946, 1952, © 1971, 1973 by the
Division of Christian Education of the National
Council of the Churches of Christ in the USA

Cover photo by Graham Holder
Illustrations by Rita Hobbs

*Cover photo shows Rob & Marion with
their children Jo, Debbie and Naomi*

Printed in Great Britain for
KINGSWAY PUBLICATIONS LTD
Lottbridge Drove, Eastbourne, E.Sussex BN23 6NT by
Richard Clay (The Chaucer Press) Ltd, Bungay, Suffolk.
Typeset by Nuprint Services Ltd, Harpenden, Herts.

Contents

To
Jo, Debbie and Naomi
without whom
there would have been little to
say

Preface

Who would be stupid enough to write a book about family and church and how they fit together, seeing that many family secrets would have to be revealed in the process?

Well, we have been! And, actually, we've enjoyed it. We wanted to be as honest as possible, so we haven't disguised too many things. One of the results, I suppose, is that some people might think that our family sounds more ideal than real. I can assure you that it is not! There have been times when, while writing, Marion and I have stopped and asked ourselves whether we really practise what we pen. We thought that one of the acid tests would be to see if the children agreed with what we had written.

I have to confess that Marion did most of the work, writing the majority of the chapters. However, we both scrutinized each other's chapters and wouldn't let anything go by without absolute agreement. So in a very real sense we wrote the book together, but special thanks to Marion for the hours and hours of putting pen to paper.

Special thanks too to Don Field, Marion's father, who gave much time in casting an expert eye over grammar and punctuation and who skilfully typed the manuscript. Other thanks go to our friends who provided the cover photo and chapter title illustrations, and to a friend called Ishmael who provided some good ideas and who has had a real ministry to our children, as indeed he has to many, many others.

We have by no means learnt all there is to know about family and church life, but we are trusting that God will use what we have written to help, guide and encourage.

ROB WHITE

1. Look Who's Talking!

MARION

'Shall we put all our dirty washing into one basket?' It didn't take me too long to realize that the tall, good-looking young man lounging on the sofa beside me was actually making a marriage proposal. Although it wasn't the most romantic proposal I'd ever heard, it was certainly different, and I decided without hesitation to accept.

I remember Rob saying before we were married that Crawley was a good place to live because his work area stretched from Reigate to Brighton. I was unconvinced because all my middle-class upbringing told me that Crawley was a new town and totally lacking in character. However, we both liked the house he had found, and that was where we were to begin our married life. The twelve years that we spent in Crawley were very happy and I still look on it as home. I think it gave us the cultural jolt that we needed.

Rob very soon took on the youth work at Three Bridges Free Church, so our house was constantly full of young people. It was a joy to find people from many different backgrounds who were so friendly and not concerned with the status seeking we had grown up with in the middle-class suburbia of Surrey.

I remember being amazed that the neighbours in our street had rows in public and thought nothing of letting the whole street know how they felt. One husband pushed his wife down the stairs and she had to go to hospital and we all heard it going on. Our sheltered upbringing had taught us that if you had disagreements you never let the neighbours hear anything!

We discovered that one couple in our road were recently married, had moved from Surrey, and that the husband had even gone to the same school as Rob. We formed an immediate friendship. Both the wife and I became pregnant around the same time.

Nobody picked up on the fact that I was very large early in my pregnancy and the possibility of twins wasn't mentioned until I went for a check-up at thirty-four weeks. People in the church rallied round and within a week we had all we needed for two babies instead of one!

We moved house when the twins, Joanna and Deborah, were nine months old. We had begun to climb the ladder of success. Bigger house, more money, more material things. In the church Rob was still youth leader, but had also become a deacon.

It was at this point that we became aware that, while our youth group consisted of nice churchy young people, there were many young people in Crawley who were completely unchurched and had no contact whatsoever with Christians. At that time one of the major problems in Crawley was drug-taking. We decided to have a coffee-bar-type outreach and managed to book the Youth Wing of a large comprehensive school. We invited a team called 'In the Name of Jesus' to lead the outreach, with someone called Clive Calver as their leader. . . .

There was a tremendous response and we found ourselves trying to cram eighty-plus young people into our house for meetings—many new Christians and many young people from unhappy home situations, some seeking to find a solution to their problems by taking drugs or dabbling in the occult.

In a matter of weeks we had gained a thriving young people's work with many encouragements and many difficulties; young people needing to talk and needing our time. Rob found he could no longer lead this group on his personality alone. They needed to know the reality of God in their lives. There was one young man within the youth group, Graham, who was able to help them in a way that we could not. He had a relationship with God that was beyond our experience, despite the fact that both of us had been brought up in Christian homes and had been Christians for many years. God was so real to Graham. The fact was that he cared about people and could discern their needs in a way that we could not. Rob and I began to feel powerless and useless. It was at this point that God met us in a new way and filled us with his Holy Spirit.

A few months before this Rob had changed his job for the third time. He was now buyer and manager of a perfumery department in the country's fourth-largest store, with a staff of twenty-five glamorous beauty consultants. Looking back now, he reckons that was ideal training for dealing with people and their problems!

With an interesting job, good prospects of promotion and an increased salary, we were now set to move to a bigger house. We tried many times to sell, but each time the transaction fell through. We were also feeling overwhelmed by the constant flow of young people in and out of our house most of the day. We thought if we moved slightly further out of Crawley we would lose some of the time-wasters. At least that was our excuse! It became increasingly clear to us, however, that God didn't seem to agree with our plans! What was he trying to show us?

One very memorable day we were visiting my parents and then Rob's. We were driving the four miles in between the two homes when we actually voiced aloud to each other the growing awareness that God was calling us to open our home to have people in need living with us as part of our family. It took nearly two years from that day until the call came to fruition, with much heartache and prayer.

The greatest opposition we had was from our Christian friends. I remember one of the deacons from Three Bridges telling Rob that he thought he was wrong to contemplate doing this kind of work, because I was not strong enough physically or emotionally, and would not be able to take the pressure. He felt certain that the children would suffer as well. I think humanly speaking, that assumption would have been correct, but it didn't allow for the supernatural power of God that overrules our logic and reason.

The greatest encouragement to us was that the elders of Three Bridges supported us in recognizing God's call on our lives. Rob's mother, particularly, gave us much spiritual encouragement.

The most difficult thing was for Rob to give up work. It meant letting go of our material security and stepping into the unknown. It was Rob's Jewish boss at work who probably helped him most at this time. He asked him why he was hesitating when it was so obvious that his greatest desire was to serve God and care for people. Rob couldn't answer that, so he handed in his resignation. (No, the boss wasn't trying to get rid of him!)

At this time we had no one living with us, and only our three-bedroomed house, but the day Rob left work he arrived home with a needy young man he had met at the railway station. He stayed for the week-end, and on the Sunday night we received a phone-call from friends asking if we could help a young girl who had arrived on their doorstep in great distress. This was the start of our extended family and for nearly a year we lived in very cramped conditions; the rather hysterical young girl sleeping on a bed-settee in the lounge, later to be joined by a 6' 2" amply-proportioned, awkward German fellow, who slept wall to wall in the dining room. Occasionally we gained a Nigerian in the kitchen at week-ends!

We moved into 'Open House', a large nine-bed-roomed Victorian house in Crawley, in November 1975. Graham and Marian, the young man from the youth group and his new wife, moved in with us to help. By this time we had gained a third daughter, Naomi, who was fifteen months. The twins were now four-and-a-half years old.

Our first Christmas there was another memorable occasion. As well as the hysterical young girl and the awkward German, we had taken in an alcoholic and a drug-addict. Throughout all the difficult times at 'Open House' the one thing we hung on to was that God had called us, and he would enable us.

During these years we saw a community church established in Crawley, called the Vine Fellowship. It was very difficult to leave Three Bridges, but after a number of increasingly frustrating years, we knew that it was right to go. I am glad to say, however, that we continued to have an open and loving relationship with the leadership there.

Seeing the Fellowship develop was a very exciting time. We experienced the reality of true friendship, sharing and caring for one another. Initially the Fellowship was made up of young couples with young children, and young single people. Rob and I knew that we could count on these folk to give us practical and spiritual support. If necessary people would come to our assistance in 'Open House' at any time of the day or night. One of the single girls, Heather, left her job as an occupational therapist and moved in to join us, taking on the role of housekeeper.

By the summer of 1980 we knew that change was in the air. Two or three of our friends had told Rob that they felt his ministry needed to be wider, and he himself sensed a growing awareness that God was drawing him beyond the four walls of 'Open House', and the demands of the local fellowship.

It was at this point in time that Clive Calver appeared on the scene again! He called in to see us and talked to Rob about the possibility of him working for Youth for Christ. In an amazing way everything came together, and by September 1980 Rob was Centres Liaison Director for YFC. We were given a home in

Crawley for a year by some good friends, and we moved out of 'Open House'.

As a family, life was completely different. All Naomi had ever known was a daddy at home all day, and now he was sometimes away for days at a time. The year in Crawley was one of readjustment. We realized that the work in 'Open House' had exhausted us, but it was a unique time of seeing God changing people's lives. We learnt so many lessons by our mistakes, but our faith was greatly enlarged.

In August 1981 we moved back to Surrey, to Rob's birthplace and only three miles from my own. How strange it was to be back in the area we had lived in before our marriage, but to feel so differently about it.

It was good to be able to experience once again the joys and problems that come from being an individual family unit in our own family home, although the children certainly missed—and still miss—that sense of community that comes from living with others.

Again we have seen a new fellowship start and grow, but this time so different from Crawley—the surroundings are different, the culture is different and the people are different; yet there is that same hunger to see the reality of God in individual and church life. During this time in Banstead a new national director was needed in British Youth for Christ and, much to our amazement, Rob was eventually invited to accept the position. The two words that we used as we faced all the new responsibilities both began with 'H'— 'Hallelujah' and 'Help'!

So that's why we've written this book! It has been through these differing circumstances with their times of excitement and of discouragement that we have seen our family life develop and deepen; with the great joy of seeing the children involved in kingdom business as well as ourselves. It has by no means been easy but, as we look back, there are several things which we believe we have learnt. So as you read on you can know that you are dealing neither with theoreticians, nor supersaints just ordinary people who have come along a certain way and wish to share some of the lessons learnt through both failure and success.

2. Happy Families

MARION

There is a children's card game entitled 'Happy Families', which I remember from my own childhood. Families of animals had to be collected together, and there was for example, Mr & Mrs Hedgehog, Master Hedgehog, and Miss Hedgehog. A warm, cosy, friendly picture of a family, and yet nowadays it seems so far removed from the true picture of the average family. Families seem to spend more time being divided than together, and many families are incomplete because one parent has left home.

What an opportunity for us as Christian families to be a true example of a 'Happy Family'. Not just the sort of happiness that is put on when you smile for a family photograph (even for the cover of a book!), but a truly happy, contented, fulfilled family, that enjoys being together and has a bond of love between all the members. Jesus said, 'Where two or three have gathered together in My name, there I am in their midst' (Mt 18:20). As a family we can be a visible demonstration of his church in our town, our street and to our neighbours. Although indeed we are part of the larger family of God we still have our own smaller family identity, and Jesus promises that he will be in our midst.

It should be pointed out that one of Satan's biggest strategies has been to break down the family unit. God intentionally created the first family, and put people into a family unit. And no wonder, since before the beginning of time God has existed as a perfect fellowship between three persons. So many scriptural principles are based on the concept of the family. If Satan successfully destroyed the idea of the institution of the family, we would have no reference point from which to begin to understand the Bible. Those of you who have been involved in counselling will know how much harder it is for someone who has never known parents, or parents' love, to understand God as their Father.

The latest developments with test-tube babies, surrogate mothers and sperm banks continue to destroy the biblical concept of the family. Divorce is becoming easier all the time and many young people go into marriage on the understanding that, if it doesn't work out, they can easily obtain a divorce. Many don't even bother to get married in the first place. The security of the family is ebbing away. The absence of absolutes, authority, moral standards and norms has fathered a society which itself is now, ever more openly, bringing those very things to birth, thereby perpetuating a grotesque travesty of the perfect world that God created.

It is within this context that the Christian family finds itself. We are right in the thick of a spiritual battle. As Paul writes in Ephesians 6:12, 'Our struggle is not against flesh and blood, but against the rulers, against the powers, against the world forces of this darkness, against the spiritual *forces* of wickedness in the heavenly places.' If you have never entered into spiritual warfare you need to ask God to open your eyes to the battle that is raging around your family at this particular moment in time. Do not despair though, the glorious fact is that with Jesus in the midst we have his authority to combat the enemy and win a resounding victory.

The world is looking to see lived out examples of good family life. People stop and take notice when they see something that works. As Larry Christenson comments in his book *The Christian Family* (page 200),

> This is the opportunity which lies before us as Christian families—to so experience the reality and power of Christ in our homes, to so live according to His Divine Order, that those around us can see that something has happened.

When we experience that reality in our families it makes us natural witnesses. Before we embark on the latest programme for evangelism in our churches we should consider afresh the ready-made programme that is in our homes and families.

It is usually harder to get people who aren't Christians to come to something organized in a church building, than it is to invite them into our homes, especially if we have spent time getting to know them and building up friendships. It is a sad thing that when people become Christians they usually have quite a wide circle of non-Christian friends, but as time goes by that circle decreases until sometimes all their friends are Christian. They stick together for support and friendship, not daring to venture out of their cloister, unless there is a particular evangelistic outreach, when they dash out, grab some poor unsuspecting victim, and then retreat quickly to the safety of the church fellowship. But it is far less threatening to be able to invite people into our own home— both for them and for us.

There are specific opportunities for evangelism in the home which we can utilize. Christmas is a time when we can invite neighbours into our home. We can then either make it a social event or talk about the real meaning of Christmas, with perhaps a time of carol-singing, as well as some of the other Christmas traditions. In Banstead we have enjoyed going out singing carols in the streets. Some of our neighbours have joined in with us and have been quite amazed that we were doing it for the joy of it, and not for the money!

The most important witness though is not the one-off events, but how we go about our daily lives. People notice more than we think, and it matters far more how we behave at home than how good, sweet and holy we look sitting in a church pew. Unfortunately most of our neighbours never darken the doors of a church, and they only see our reactions when the car won't start, when we lock ourselves out, or when their ball comes over our fence for the two-hundredth time!

Since we have lived in Banstead it is really our children, rather than us, who have been involved in the more direct evangelism. The twins have seen quite a few of their school friends become Christians, and have had good talks with many of our neighbours. They have a boldness which puts us to shame. Rob and I are often called in to follow up what they have initiated. None of our children are embarrassed to talk about their faith, although Naomi is shyer by nature. When we travel by train they invariably get involved in conversation before long. On the way to Spring Harvest once, two nuns came to sit by us and happened to ask the children where they were going. They were immediately given the complete low-down on Spring Harvest. The nuns seemed very interested and wanted to know if we knew anything about the charismatic renewal. We spent the next three hours sharing together and had a lovely time of fellowship with them.

For our children, Spring Harvest is one of the highlights of the year. Two years ago, on our return, Debbie was excitedly regaling one of her schoolfriends with all the details, when the friend burst into tears. She told Debbie that she wanted to know Jesus like that, whereupon Debbie prayed for her, and then told her to pray and ask Jesus into her life. I was informed about this, but to be honest, was somewhat cautious, knowing that Debbie is given to being rather dramatic. Two years on we can witness the changed life of that young girl from her conversion experience in Debbie's bedroom.

Our biggest handicap as a family is that Rob is away quite a bit, and it is difficult for him to build up relationships with the neighbours. Also as a whole family we are quite often away at weekends, when most other people are at home. Once or twice when one of our neighbours has really needed help, or someone to talk to, we haven't been available—that is something that frustrates us, and is hard to come to terms with. If we spend all our time going to church meetings, and being involved in church activities there will be no time to just be ourselves, and get to know our neighbours on a purely friendly basis. Non-Christians need to see that Christians are ordinary human beings. If we are so busy 'serving God' that we have no time to get to know our neighbours, we need to look again at our priorities. The accusations against Jesus were that he spent too much time eating with publicans and sinners, not that he went to the synagogue too often!

One of our neighbours when we lived in Crawley once commented to us, 'I can't believe you are Christians, you look so normal.' Goodness knows what her concept of a Christian was, but probably something akin to a Martian! People need to see us relaxing and behaving normally in our homes. Graham Kendrick wrote a song which says:

One shall tell another, and he shall tell his friend,
Husbands, wives and children shall come following on.
From house to house in families shall more be
    gathered in,
And lights will shine in every street, so warm and
    welcoming.

Graham Kendrick © Thankyou Music 1981

What a lovely natural way to share the gospel, and something we could all covet to come to pass in our street. We have one other Christian family four doors away from us, and it has been a source of tremendous encouragement to be able to share with them, and to pray together for our neighbours.

If we are submitted to God, and trusting him to direct our paths, each day becomes a new adventure, and we can leave him to bring people and opportunities our way. Just going to the shops provides so many possibilities for him to use us, and who knows who we will meet down the crowded gangways of Tesco's! I have often longed that just like the glow which comes from eating Readybrek (according to the advert), people would notice that the Holy Spirit is radiating through me. I confess it hasn't happened yet, but I'm praying that it will!

It is so exciting when together as a family we can share incidents that have happened to us. One of the twins got talking to a lady on the bus coming home from swimming recently, and as she talked about her faith this lady confessed that she had been a Christian, but had backslidden. Who knows what that conversation could have triggered off. Our plumber is very interested in Christian things, and we have had some really good chats over numerous cups of tea. Don't think our family is always keen to witness and talk to people, because we have missed many opportunities, but often coversations develop so naturally that there is no effort involved at all.

Being available to give practical help to our neighbours is so valuable. Doing something tangible means so much more than words alone. At times of emergency too, neighbours often turn to those people who they sense have a strength that is more than just their own—even if up to that point they haven't been interested in Christianity.

We need to discover afresh the real joy that comes from being a Christian family. With so many pressures around us, it is all too easy to get bogged down with the problems of life, and not enjoy simply being together. Children are such a tremendous source of fun and enjoyment, and we need to be able to allow them to give us pleasure. If we are too busy it is more likely that their fun will become an irritation to us. If we are constantly filling our lives with other things, our children will grow up and we will look back and wish we could redeem the time that we missed being with them.

As families we need to have 'quality' time together. It does not have to be of any particular duration, but it is that time when we lay aside our individual desires, and seek to benefit the others in some way. Maybe it will be doing a jig-saw or playing a game together, making music together, going for a walk—whatever suits your family. It is not vital to talk all the time, but as we share enjoyment of life together that lays a foundation which makes it possible to talk out deeper issues.

Mealtimes are great times for communication. Our mealtimes are noisy as we are all fairly vocal, but it is an opportunity to catch up on family news. The television has destroyed much of the communication that existed between families. We all too often use television as a means of keeping the children amused, and we relax in front of it after a busy day at work, but it is a dangerous instrument and needs to be monitored carefully. Selectivity is essential.

Occasionally it is really good for one of the parents to take one of the children out on their own and do something special together. Naomi is quiet, but when she and I, or she and Rob, are alone she talks endlessly because she doesn't have to fight with the twins to get a word in edgeways. For her it is vital to have a one-to-one relationship. Likewise, the twins—who spend so much of their time being lumped together—for different reasons appreciate individual attention.

Rob took Jo away with him recently on one of his preaching weekends. She was delighted to be able to go with him and share in his work. He was thrilled when he arrived back in his room on the Saturday evening and found a note on his bed which simply said, 'I love you very much, Daddy, and I shall be praying for you as you lead the meeting.' Both Rob and Jo had benefited from being together, and they had ample opportunity to talk together over many issues.

Discipline is an important factor to consider alongside the enjoyment of being together. There can be no joy if children call the tune, and parents lose control. (This is discussed more fully in chapter 9.) If we have sought to discipline our children from the earliest moment, it becomes easier to let them have more independence as they grow older, and for us to become friends to them, as well as parents. Obviously there are bound to be areas of difficulty, and problems that arise with the children individually, but the right foundations of discipline make a world of difference.

Rob and I are very aware, as we write this book,

that the twins are in their early teens, and the next few years may bring additional problems, but we are not pessimistic about the prospect. We know that God is well able to keep *his* children, and that if we have kept our part of the deal, which is to 'train up a child in the way he should go', we can trust him for their future. For those of us who have teenage children, and are aware of the many pressures and temptations that surround them, there are some verses in Philippians 4 which we would do well to stick by our bedside, or some other suitable place.

> Be anxious for nothing, but in everything by prayer and supplication with thanksgiving let your requests be made known to God. And the peace of God, which surpasses all comprehension, shall guard your hearts and minds in Christ Jesus. (Phil 4:6–7)

Does a worrying, nagging parent ever really achieve anything? When I think back to my own teenage years I remember deliberately going against everything my Christian parents stood for, but underneath it all I remained secure in the fact that they loved me, and that God loved me, and in the end my rebellion simply fizzled out.

It is so strange to see our own children responding in the same way as we responded all those years ago. Jo and Debbie have always got on so well together, but now suddenly they appear to pose a threat to each other. I, as their mother and also another woman, can also appear threatening. Rob hasn't fallen from his pedestal yet, but come the first real boyfriend he will soon be toppled. No longer can I as their mother simply dictate what they must do, as they can rationally argue their case, and pick on the faults and weaknesses in mine. At their age they still desperately need a mum who will hug them and continue to correct them, but they also need a friend and confidante who can come alongside.

Debbie confessed to losing her temper at school, and I immediately responded with a lecture about her lack of self-control. Her reply was, 'Well Mum it's unfortunate because I inherited my quick temper from you, and you still lose your temper sometimes!' What could I say? We are praying for each other!

So you see our family is not the ideal model, but we love one another very much, and we are prepared to weather the bad times for the joy that comes from our togetherness. In the words of Larry Christenson (*The Christian Family*, page 215): 'The Christian family reckons upon a God who is a God of battle, a God who wins victories. When God takes charge of our warfare, then we can reckon upon this promise. In his time he will strengthen and establish us in victory. 1 Pet 5:10.'

Such a family, one in which he has taken charge, will be his witness.

3. Hello Children – Goodbye Freedom?

MARION

Children are a gift of the Lord;
The fruit of the womb is a reward.
Like arrows in the hand of a warrior,
So are the children of one's youth.

Ps 127:3-4

How many of us truly appreciate God's gifts to us and see our children as a reward from God? Why is it that God's plan that we should be proud of our children and find joy and delight in them seems so often thwarted, and children are seen to be a burden, a hindrance, and a source of sadness?

I think that, before we look at the effects that having children has on us, we need to look at one overruling principle that is sometimes ignored.

It is vital to recognize that children are a *gift* from

God. This is not just for Christian parents, but for all parents. In this day and age when we can plan our family and decide how many children we want, when we want them, and one day soon choose whether we want a boy or girl, it is so easy to think that we have done it all and forget that it is only the Creator who can create.

I remember my first glimpse of our twins, and being incredibly moved by the wonder of their completeness and perfection. It still amazes me to see a new-born baby and know that only God could have made every part to come together so amazingly. How can people remain atheists after witnessing the miracle of birth? It is interesting that when God calls Jeremiah he says, 'Before I formed you in the womb I knew you, and before you were born I consecrated you.'

Once we grasp the truth that children are a gift from God, we can see that he has a responsibility for them. Just as he knew Jeremiah before he was born, before he was even formed in the womb (an interesting verse for those who think that a foetus isn't really a person until 'it' is a certain age), God knows our children before we do, and he chooses to give them to us. We have found laying hold of this truth very important and very helpful in the bringing up of our children.

I recall very well the euphoria I experienced after having Jo and Debbie which lasted throughout the ten days I was in hospital. Then I remember arriving home and slowly beginning to realize that these two babies were actually ours and that we were responsible for them. For me, particularly, it caused a crisis.

Rob and I had many theories and ideas about how

29

we would bring up our children and what we would do. One thing we were certain about was that having a child was not going to alter our lifestyle. The baby would have to fit in with us! The fact that we had two babies did throw us slightly, but we were not daunted and were still determined to pursue our original course of action. With that in mind I decided, two or three days after being home from hospital, that I would leave the twins with my mother and go out with Rob to take an evening service at a local church. I ignored my mother's mutterings about how foolish I was, and it wasn't until I returned home to give Jo and Debbie their 10 p.m. feed that it finally hit me. These babies were mine, I was their mother, I was totally responsible and I couldn't give them back. I remember sobbing uncontrollably as the reality of it all dawned upon me.

I was angry with God. How could he have allowed me to get into this mess? Rob was to blame as well. They both knew how much I loved life, and now, at only twenty-two years of age, I had lost my freedom. I fought a private battle with God that night. I find it's always better to vent your feelings on God first. He is more understanding than most!

It was as if I had hurt God's feelings. I felt he was saying to me, 'I thought you would like this gift, in fact I even gave you a double portion to enjoy! Don't forget you are not alone in this. I care about those two children of mine far more than you do.'

I was able to come to terms with the responsibility of motherhood, knowing that these children were God's first and mine second. He had entrusted them to Rob and me to bring up only by following his instructions.

That night I consciously gave our children back to God. The release was tremendous. I knew that although many demands would be made on us, and that we had a responsibility no one else could take, these children were ultimately in the hands of their Maker.

That knowledge has helped Rob and me in every aspect of bringing up our children. It underlies how we discipline them—according to their Maker's instructions. It means we value them as human beings entrusted into our care, but we don't possess them; they are on loan. When the crises come and they are seriously ill or in some kind of danger, we know that our hold on them must be light not heavy.

The effect of children on us

Many couples change drastically when they become parents. There are two different reactions. One is to become totally dedicated to this beautiful offspring who demands all their time and attention. But only God demands our total dedication. The other reaction is to become resentful and annoyed that this baby has come either between the two of them, or between them and their lifestyle, and is spoiling their relationship. In a way there is an unwillingness to take on the responsibility. The second attitude is often due to a selfish attitude in the parents, and there is probably much insecurity in the marriage. The new baby actually poses a threat to one or both of the partners.

There is definitely a change when a baby (or babies!) comes into your life. In spite of all our hunger for learning, most of us know very little about mother-hood and fatherhood until we experience it ourselves. School, college, university and secular life teach us little about what to expect when we become parents. There are many books written about baby care and child development, but not much on how to cope with your own emotions and feelings on becoming parents.

For a woman it usually means a complete change in role, as most women nowadays leave work to have their first baby, and even if they go back to work afterwards it is then as a 'working mother'. There are many changes and adjustments to make. Husbands need to realize that when a woman stops working to have children she loses her job satisfaction, and often feels that she is no longer of any value to the outside world. She depends much more on her husband for that vital sense of self-worth. Some women end up with no sense of value at all and lose their identity as it becomes submerged in being a wife and mother. Some women look to their children to fulfil them, which can be frustrating and cause bitterness as the children become independent. Women need to be aware that neither husband nor children can completely fulfil them as people, only God can; and although they want to be the best wife and mother they can be, there is no need to bury themselves in this role, never to rise again.

For a man his role as breadwinner is usually unchanged, but he becomes not only a husband but also a father, with that added responsibility for his household. It is no longer just a case of building a career, coming home at night and eating a meal, watching TV etc, or, if not too tired and reasonably in pocket, going out together. It is suddenly having to ask questions like, 'How does my work impinge on my family?' and , 'Seeing that my wife has got this major new responsibility all day, what kind of help can I give when I get home?' Painful questions have to be faced, but they are necessary ones if family life is going to be the new foundation which we build. If little Herbert, or Esmeralda, is just an extra ingredient, or novelty, or problem, or excitement in life, then family life will always be a pressure, with our continually resenting the intrusion into something which was going so well. Although we don't change our basic patterns of life to fit in with his little lordship/her little ladyship, we certainly need to realize that life will not continue in the same way that it has to date, and that new foundational considerations have to be worked out. Yes, like everything else, it costs! If you want a rich family life (God's way) you pay the price. If you don't want to pay (selfish way) you don't get the goods. Terrifyingly straightforward!

Still husband and wife

It has been said that 'the greatest gift a mother can give her child is to love the father of her child and the greatest gift a father can give his child is to love the mother of his child'. We sincerely believe that the most important advice to give to a couple who have a new baby is to work extra hard at being a husband and wife. Babies are amazingly resilient, and if you make a few mistakes in your motherhood and fatherhood along the way, it is surprising how well they survive. Our three girls have come through many harrowing experiences and still seem fairly normal. Hopefully the twins won't need healing of the memories from the time I took them shopping in their pram when they were very tiny, and on my return home realized I was without them! And I don't think their lack of academic brilliance can be put down to the fact that, when they were small, they all rolled off the bed on to the floor at one time or another.

Most couples reckon the hardest thing is to find time for one another. The new routine of nappies and feeds is both demanding and exhausting. Communication is the most important thing. You need to say how you feel, and to be honest with one another. Most men are very good about helping with the new baby. Rob was wonderful, though he did avoid changing dirty nappies if at all possible! Men need to realize that their wives are likely to be rather emotional, prone to bursting into tears at the slightest thing, very worried if the baby shows any sign of anything being wrong, and often too tired to enjoy anything—even love-making.

Women need to realize that most men have come home after a hard day at work, being surrounded by any number of attractive girls who don't look tired and haggard, smell of sick, or have a screaming baby tucked under one arm. Women can often make too many demands on their menfolk, so that in the end they enjoy going out to that boring church meeting just to have a breather. Also it helps if a wife's vocabulary is a little more extensive than babies, feeds, nappies, wind, etc. Wives need to have other interests and to keep in touch with the outside world. It is something that calls for effort on their part, but is very necessary. It is good to get out of the house and visit friends and relatives, or just to go for a walk. It is also worth remembering that husbands need to be listened to too!

It is not our belief that children today need as much attention as all the books say we should give them. It is true that every child is an individual human being, so his needs will vary and it is impossible to generalize. But our biggest fault today is that we overstimulate our children with too much, and it ends in them being bored. Also having smaller families means that the attention is far more on the individual children. The main needs of our children are love, security, warmth, food and sleep, which are not difficult to provide.

Two of our friends have made a point of going out together once a week for a meal ever since the birth of their son. Where you go for a meal obviously depends on what you can afford, but we have a very good Happy Eater in Banstead! It is not what you do together that matters, but the fact that you deliberatley carve out time for one another.

Effect on our relationship with God

Our relationship with God often suffers after the arrival of our first child and continues to suffer while the children are small. Firstly, it is necessary to face the fact that the relationship will probably need to be maintained in a different way from before, simply because of the change in daily routine.

For men it may not be so different, although Rob found it difficult to maintain his time with God in the morning, after a broken night's sleep and the usual morning rush. He discovered that he could pray while driving the car, and that is something that has developed over the years which he now values immensely. If you see him driving up the M1 with eyes closed and hands raised, give him plenty of room!

I found I was too tired in the morning to read my Bible or pray. However, there were other times in the day when I had to sit still, for example, when I was feeding the twins, and those times were opportunities to pray. When the baby is asleep is a good opportunity to read the Bible—before you start tearing around catching up on the housework! It is very beneficial for us to have these times of quiet and rest in the midst of a busy life, as we very rarely sit still at any other time.

Our relationship with God needs to be continually deepening and growing, and we must work hard at making that a priority, and not something we fit in if we have the time.

The greatest hindrance to my relationship with God in the early years of our marriage was not the children, but my obsession with keeping the house clean and tidy; a proud attitude that even with twins my house always had to look immaculate! It took me quite some time to realize how much I was missing out on, and to see that people felt far more relaxed in a homely, if slightly untidy, environment, than one that was spotless but lacking in warmth and homeliness.

One of my old schoolfriends, who moved to Crawley and started coming to our fellowship, wasn't and still isn't the most organized of people. However, she and her husband have two lovely children, and their home has a really relaxed atmosphere. Rita always has time to talk and listen to people that come into it. I don't think God is too worried about a few specks of dust. Fortunately for us he cares more about people!

The story of Martha and Mary is one that leaves us feeling sorry for Martha, who worked so hard, and annoyed with Mary who just sat at the feet of Jesus. But Jesus says in Luke 10:41, 'Martha, Martha, you are worried and bothered about so many things; but *only* a few things are necessary, really *only* one, for Mary has chosen the good part, which shall not be taken away from her.'

Babies and church

It is sadly true that couples who have never sorted out what commitment to Christ really means, gradually drift away from the life of the church once they have children. When I use the word 'church' I don't mean a building, but a group of God's people meeting together in a locality. Unfortunately it is also possible to begin to drift even if you are at first committed. When I look back over the lives of many young people we know who were really on fire for God, eager to go wherever he sent them, and to turn the world upside down, it makes me both sad and angry to see those same young people marry, become parents, and settle down into a mediocre, safe, secure, comfortable existence that isn't going to be of any use to God. Having children is no excuse for adopting a safe position and an attitude of complacency!

From the moment of birth our children are part of the church, and we need to begin to integrate them into the life of the church from that point in time. There is much that is wrong in the church's attitude to children in this country, which we will say more about in chapter 4, but that is no reason to opt out of being part of it, and of working together for change. We need to see the importance of children in our midst in the same way as Jesus saw them. 'Let the children come to me, and do not hinder them; for to such belongs the kingdom of heaven' (Mt 19:14 RSV).

Most churches have a crêche during the morning service so that parents with babies can worship together at least once a week. It is not a bad thing for babies to be looked after by somebody different, and to see other children of a similar age.

It may be that your child happens to sleep in the morning, and you don't want to upset his routine, but often that is just an excuse for not going to the service yourself. Mothers are more prone to hide behind their children than fathers, and because we still have an attitude among many men within the church that it is a woman's duty to be at home, we get away with it! If we truly are part of the body of Christ, then we are denying our brothers and sisters that part if we don't meet with them. Every one of us is vitally necessary. Babies can stand having their routine changed occasionally.

The other excuse I often hear is that there is a lack of trust in whoever is running the crêche, therefore a reluctance to leave the child with them. Surely we need more honesty with one another if we truly have worries in this area, although it is worth bearing in mind that most mothers with a first child are more likely to be overprotective towards them.

Other friends in the church can help by baby-sitting occasionally, so that both parents can go to the evening service. It isn't easy to adjust to one parent going out without the other to meetings, and Rob and I have been very grateful to so many people who have been prepared to look after our children to enable us to be together.

Rob and I have always endeavoured to take our children with us as much as possible. When they were little they would happily sleep in their carrycots anywhere, and today they certainly have no problems about sleeping in strange beds, on the floor, or in very strange surroundings. As long as children feel secure they don't usually mind where they sleep. Children who are treated too delicately usually behave too delicately.

It is sometimes helpful to offer to have mid-week meetings in your own home, so that again you have the opportunity of being together. Obviously if there are many couples in the same boat in your church, you can take turns.

Most of all the desire to meet with God and his people needs to be so strong that it overrides the practical problems of how this can be achieved.

The blessings children bring

We have covered the more negative effects that having children brings, but it would be good to look at some of the many positive consequences of the arrival of children.

The sheer joy of seeing your child for the first time is incomparable. A tiny human being, created by God, but conceived through the physical union of husband and wife. A visible reminder that the two 'shall become one flesh'.

Let us look at some of those special moments that those of us who are parents treasure for life:

When our baby responds to us with his first smile.

When he holds out his arms to us as his mum and dad.

When he takes his first faltering steps towards us.

When he says spontaneously 'I love you Daddy' or 'I love you Mummy'.

Every stage of development continues to have those moments that we treasure so much.

Children have a zest for life, boundless energy, and an irrepressible desire to discover more about the world around them. Whem my mum was dying of cancer, I would come home after a day's visit, feeling sad and heavy-hearted, and walk into the normality of the girls having fun together, chattering about the day's events, with a childish unawareness of the seriousness of life and death. Seeing them helped to keep me sane and able to cope with what seemed like a nightmarish situation.

What pride we have as parents when little Phyllis gets a three-word part in the school play, or comes first in the egg and spoon race on Sports Day. I remember seeing Jo and Debbie dressed as angels in their first school nativity play. There was a lump in my throat and tears in my eyes. This summer on Sports Day Naomi, with no previous form, came from the back to take third place in the 400 metres. I glowed with pride!

Doesn't it give us a glimpse of how God feels about

us? Somehow, once we are parents it gives us more insight into the fatherhood of God—how much he loves us, how his heart swells with pride over us, how we give him so much joy, despite our faults and failings. 'He will exult over you with joy, He will be quiet in His love, He will rejoice over you with shouts of joy' (Zeph 3:17).

How many times have you, who are parents, crept into your children's bedrooms at night and seen them sleeping peacefully, looking so perfect, so angelic, so serene? Even when you consider how naughty they have been all day, don't you regret those angry words and quick reactions?

Children are quick to respond to us, quick to forgive, and slow to bear a grudge. They are often sensitive to our needs. Their response to us makes all the demands and sacrifice worth while.

How many mums have enjoyed the luxury of breakfast in bed on Mother's Day? Forget the fact that the fried egg was cold and solid, the bacon was practically cinders, and the fried bread resembled a piece of leather—it's the thought that counts. . .

How many fathers look forward to a rapturous welcome as they walk through the front door at the end of a busy day?

Rob and I can vouch for the fact that although our daughters have caused us to age more rapidly—and probably will in the future—they are worth every exhausting, exhilarating minute of the process!

4. Sack the Sunday School?

MARION

At that time the disciples came to Jesus, saying, 'Who then is greatest in the kingdom of heaven?' And He called a child to Himself and stood him in their midst.

Mt 18:1–2

There is still a large proportion of the church in this nation who, either consciously or subconsciously, think that men are first-rate, women are second-rate and children are fifth-rate. It is encouraging to see the change coming in the way the church views women, but it is sad that up to this present time there has been little change in the way we view the children. This includes all denominations, and even the newer house fellowships and community churches have done little to change the position, or lack of it, that children have within the church.

If the above verse is true and children represent so clearly those who are the greatest in the kingdom of heaven, why do we mostly ignore their gifts and callings, keep them in the Sunday School out of the way, and then expect them to adjust instantly to the adult worship and life of the church at about fourteen years old? Is it really surprising that so many teenagers become disillusioned and fall away from the church? Jesus makes it abundantly clear to his disciples that he thinks children are important, and that they have a very special place in his heart. When the mothers brought their children to him so that he could lay hands on them and pray for them, the disciples' reaction is fairly typical of how we still react today. 'Oh, but Jesus has got far more important things to cope with; we need his time and attention, you take your children away!'

Jesus tells them to allow the children to come to him and not to hinder them, 'for the kingdom of heaven belongs to such as these' (Mt 19:13–15). We often write off these statements of Jesus as pictorial language to illustrate a parable, but let's look again! I would venture to suggest that if there is anything that the church is guilty of, and that God holds us accountable for, it is the way we have ignored the role of our children within the church. Children are not the church of tomorrow, they are the church!

We love it when at the Sunday School Anniversary all the children, dressed in their best clothes, parade into the church and have their special service. They may sing a couple of very sweet children's hymns, and then there is an animated children's talk given by a visiting speaker, who has to make sure he gets in a special word for any parents who may be there and who aren't Christians! It is a day when all the parents can be proud of their offspring; in fact when all is said and done it is really more a parents' day than a children's day.

Jesus continues in Matthew 18:6 to say that if any of us causes a child who believes in him to stumble, it would be better if we had a millstone hung round our necks and were drowned. That sounds a bit strong! Jesus is so loving and surely he can't really mean actually drowned—but he does! What's more he says it should be a heavy millstone and that we should go down into the depth of the sea. Doesn't it make you shudder a little?

Yes, but you see, children really are rather a nuisance in the church. Imagine being one of the disciples and standing in front of Jesus saying that. What do you think his reaction would be? We feel that it is so much better for children to have something geared for their own age, so we have a Sunday School. Although they have to go to school five days a week anyway, we seem to think they will enjoy going again on a Sunday. Sunday School usually happens at the same time as the morning service. That means there are other people, usually young people, who miss the morning meeting because they are teaching our children what we as Christian parents ought to be teaching them at home.

I am putting the case in an extreme form because we need to seriously rethink much of what has become tradition and habit. I realize there are practical problems when children join us for worship—especially during the sermon! But we need to remember that when Robert Raikes, a journalist from Gloucester, founded the first Sunday School in 1780, it was simply because he was concerned for children who could not read or write. He used the Bible as a book from which they learnt to read. There has been a gradual change over the last hundred years to where the Sunday School is as we know it today. The Sunday School used to be separate from the church, but that is not so much the case these days. There must be an openness amongst us to look honestly at what has been done in the church for so long, and see where it needs to change. What met a need two hundred years ago doesn't necessarily today.

There is no doubt that there is a real benefit in children being able to meet together for fellowship, enjoyment and teaching. Also, there is a case for teaching children who come from non-Christian homes, although our evangelism needs to concentrate more on families, rather than just the adults or the children. It seems we miss out on the tremendous togetherness of families being able to worship together, and the best time for that is obviously a Sunday morning. Children's meetings or clubs could be run at other times during the week.

What about the Family Service? Our experience has been that parents and adults usually sit in the main body of the church, and the children sit together as part of the Sunday School—sometimes going out after the first twenty minutes. There is usually a special hymn for the children and a children's talk, but the whole objective of having a Family Service, and being together as families worshipping God side by side, is not achieved.

45

We are so quick to sectionalize what we do, and the children's section is definitely different from the adult section. Children should be allowed the opportunity of being part of something that is designed for everyone, not one or the other.

Some house fellowships have reacted against the old traditions, and have decided to do away with Sunday School. They keep the children in the meeting all the time, which seems like a step in the right direction, but unfortunately although the children are now with their parents, the worship is still for the adults. This results in children who are spectators in a praise and worship meeting, and most of the time (usually a long time), what is happening goes right over their heads, and they are bored stiff. And of course they don't mind advertising the fact!

Christian parents seem particularly keen to disown their children. Is it that discipline is a problem, and they don't want their little terror to show them up in front of all their Christian friends? We need a good deal more honesty in our relationships with one another. We must allow our children to be themselves, and if they are particularly naughty we mustn't immediately feel failures, and condemn ourselves and the children. I often think the children of Ministers and full-time Christian workers come off worst, because they are expected to be what they definitely are not, by their parents and by others. The very pressure of expectation usually makes them ten times worse anyway!

Although it sounds rather a strong thing to say, it sometimes appears that Christian children are in danger of being neglected. Dad may have a dynamic ministry, which means he is out at different meetings most nights of the week, and when he is at home he needs time to study and to prepare. Mum may feel miffed that Dad's always out, so she goes out whenever she can, and she certainly doesn't want to be lumbered with the children all the time. Within the context of the church there is no real recognition of their worth, so it could be that we end up with our children needing ministry for problems of neglect and rejection.

In Matthew 18:10 Jesus goes on to say, 'Do not despise one of these little ones, for I say to you, that their angels in heaven continually behold the face of My Father who is in heaven.' Matthew is the only gospel to record that verse, but it is I believe a lovely glimpse of the host of angels particularly designated to watch over our children. Sometimes when we see that look of complete trust on our child's face, maybe there is some significance in the fact that their angels are constantly looking at God.

If, as Jesus says, we need to become like children to enter the kingdom of heaven, it seems obvious that we need to watch and learn from them. Children have a natural humility. It is our influence as parents that teaches them otherwise. They have no trouble forgiving and forgetting. They don't bear grudges. They have a high level of openness and honesty. Their lives aren't full of hang-ups. Bitterness, jealousy, resentment, anger and pride have not taken a hold, and they are more able to see God clearly because their vision is not blurred.

When Jo and Debbie were two years old we used to have meetings of praise and worship in our house with the young people in our church. The twins would hear the singing and creep out of bed and sit on the stairs. If you looked up you would see two figures in nighties with eyes closed and hands raised, a look of serenity on their faces. Maybe they were just copying others, maybe they were too young to understand, but who knows! They were certainly enjoying themselves.

It is a fact that children can come into a relationship with Jesus when they are very young. It may be limited, it may lack understanding, but there is a definite relationship. We must think very carefully before we put our children off becoming Christians, even if we do think they are too young to understand. It could be that we are being a stumbling block.

When the fellowship in Crawley started, we went through many different stages of thinking about the children, and how they could be more integrated into the life of the church. It was not until we moved to Banstead that the ideas were more formulated as far as their involvement was concerned. We arrived in Banstead with three children of ten, ten and seven, who had never been to a Sunday School, and who were used to times of open worship, participation in the singing, dancing, playing of instruments, etc. There was nothing of that kind in Banstead at that time, and we did not want to take what we felt would be a retrograde step by sending our children to a more traditional Sunday School. We prayed much about what to do and, while looking for the right local church expression to join, were invited by a widower and his two sons, to bring the children to their house on a Sunday morning. They had had many years' experience as Sunday School Superintendent and

Sunday School teachers in a local church, as well as experience in large children's missions. The idea was to encourage the children and to make it a special time for them. It caught on fast, and gradually other families and single people joined us. Now we have become Banstead Fellowship, but the Sunday morning meeting is particularly for the children, and adults enjoy joining in.

It has been a learning experience for all of us, and we are still trying different things to find out how we can best work and worship together as children and adults. We have learnt by our mistakes, and we are continually longing for our children to enjoy all that God intends them to enjoy. It has been necessary for the adults to make a conscious decision to sacrifice some of their own desires for the sake of the children. Actually we have found that those needs and desires are often met through the children, in what they say and do. We also have mid-week house groups where the adults can share and fellowship together. We count it a real privilege for us and our children to have been involved in this experiment, and a real joy for us as parents to see our children enjoying and participating in worship with us. There are so many ways in which children of all ages can be part of our expression of church, and I shall attempt to summarize some that have been part of our experience.

To hear children praying together with the adults is perhaps one of the most exciting and moving experiences we have discovered. Children pray with absolute honesty. They get right to the point, and they don't dress up their prayers with nice phrases. They mean business with God, and they expect answers.

Sometimes God uses one of the children to pray a prayer that breaks into someone's life and brings repentance, and at other times their prayers undoubtedly have a prophetic edge. It is quite moving when one of the four year old boys prays out loud for his daddy who is ill in bed. It is also an encouragement for the adults to join with him in praying for his healing.

Recently we have spent some time in the fellowship praying for one of the twelve year old girls who has a very bad hare-lip and cleft palate. She was due to commence a course of surgery and treatment to try and rectify the problem. To witness the children join with us in laying on of hands and praying for her healing quite spontaneously was a real joy. One of the other teenage girls prayed a most beautiful prayer over her that definitely came directly from God's heart.

Children are quick to respond, and sometimes after listening to some Bible teaching they will want to pray and confess things in their lives that are wrong and don't correspond with what they have heard. Their openness has often brought the same response of confession and repentance from adults, who would probably have kept quiet about it if just left to themselves. We have seen in a very real way the outworking of James 5:16 where it says, 'Confess your sins to one another, and pray for one another, so that you may be healed.'

The other Sunday I noticed two of the children with their arms around one another quietly crying together. Only God knows what healing was being brought about through that experience, but it called to mind how we are encouraged to 'rejoice with those who rejoice, and weep with those who weep' (Rom 12:15). Sometimes our children are more sensitive to the Spirit of God than we realize—sometimes more sensitive than we are ourselves. The first time one of our daughters broke down in a meeting Rob and I were very worried. She was only four at the time, and just when we were really praising God she began to sob. It got so bad that I had to tke her out of the meeting. This happened three weeks running—when we began to praise God she burst into tears. Her only comment was how good God was and how naughty she was, and gradually it dawned on us that she was feeling convicted in the presence of God. We were able to help her to an awareness of what was going on in her young life, and were able to pray with her about it, and there was the sort of release that normally we would only expect to see in adults. How good to have a context in which such reality can be expressed!

In a similar way children sometimes have major doubts and questions about their faith. It is good to have a place where they can voice the doubts and raise the questions, and where other adults, apart from their parents, can come alongside to give their views and share their own testimonies. The first time Jo openly disagreed with Rob in a meeting, and admitted she couldn't believe what he believed because of certain doubts, I was quite stunned, but the benefit of others coming alongside, for her and for us, was tremendous. Parents of teenage children particularly may find them difficult to cope with, and yet suffer silently. It is so much better to be able to share our worries, fears and difficulties with others who really love our children too. The single people in our fellowship have been a real help to the children also. They have taken an interest in them, and been prepared to spend time with them. As families together it has been really beneficial to get to know each other's children well.

God gives his gifts to us indiscriminately, and there is no age barrier. Children can minister to others in the same way as adults, and often far more powerfully. We have witnessed children speaking in tongues, praying for healing, having words of wisdom (or knowledge) and visions. The glorious thing is that children don't pigeonhole what God does, and they don't ask questions. They simply allow God to use them. We spend so much time as adults being cautious, weighing what we are doing, and making sure our doctrine is correct. When Peter jumped out of the boat to walk on the water to Jesus, he didn't stop to check whether it had ever been done before, or whether it was allowed, he just wanted to get to Jesus. Children have a similar attitude. If they make mistakes we as adults are there to correct and advise. We expect our children to demonstrate the fruit of the Spirit when they become Christians, so there is no reason why they shouldn't receive and use the gifts of the Spirit too.

Ishmael, a singer very popular with children and creator of the 'Glories', tells how when he was a pastor of a church he stood up one Sunday to lead a time of worship, and felt so depressed that he couldn't go on and so sat down again. There was silence in the church, broken only by the deacons conferring about what they should do, and what was the matter with the pastor. As everyone sat waiting a boy of eleven got up out of the congregation, went up to Ishmael and prayed over him. God spoke through that boy, and Ishmael was restored and able to continue.

More than anything, it often seems, children love times of praise. They are uninhibited, free and spontaneous. They dance, sing, shout, clap and play instruments, and it is tremendously encouraging for the adults. They don't just have to sing children's choruses. They understand what praise is and they enjoy it. Worship is not quite so easy for them, but it is something they can be taught and led into. It is lovely to see Mum and Dad dancing with their children. Debbie, one of the twins, loves to dance. She and I don't always see eye to eye, and once, while praying about the relationship between us, I felt God urging me to dance with her. I discovered that dancing with her brought an instant mending of the relationship and a togetherness that we didn't experience any other way.

It's not just girls who enjoy the dance in our fellowship, sometimes the boys lead the way. They have an exuberance about them which is infectious.

For children who are musical, playing instruments of all varieties helps to involve them in the praise and worship. I watched one of the two year olds in the fellowship the other week, walk across the room to pick up a maraca which he then shook vigorously during the rest of the worship time—noisy, yes, but he was involved and participating!

Children are not the church of tomorrow, they are the church.

5. Let Sleeping Dads Lie

ROB

How about Dad's role in this glorious family thing? Are dads best described as masters, friends, guides, bosses, servants, or what? Perhaps they can best be looked at in terms of being carers—those entrusted with the care of a wife and children.

'Christianity begins at home' is an expression we know well, but all too often our Christianity stops at home. Home becomes a place where we let out all our pent-up frustrations, tempers and worries, often to the detriment of family life. Dad comes in from work, frayed at the edges, to find his wife frayed on the inside, and the children completely unfrayed and ready for a spirited romp! Not the best recipe for harmonious living! And it is a good thing that we can have a place where our deepest feelings can be expressed, or we would all explode emotionally, spiritually and physically. If family life is strong then each member can feel safe about displaying at times those emotions so often just under the surface.

Do I care enough for my family to allow them to express themselves sometimes in a way that may seem other than comfortable to me? But, more importantly, do I care enough for my family not to make them suffer for my selfish outbursts? The Scripture speaks of loving our wives, respecting our husbands, and not exasperating our children. We are admonished, in 1 Peter 3:8, to be harmonious, sympathetic, brotherly and kind-hearted, yet so often we ignore the needs of those closest to us, and act selfishly. We need ruthlessly to examine our lives at home to see if we are guilty of care*less* attitudes. Someone can be thought of as a very loving and caring person by others in general, but can be a brute at home. Surely that is hypocritical, and the balance should be redressed so that home is the place where love and care are initially demonstrated.

Now this matter of care at home is often quite difficult for us fathers to put into practice. We seem to have tried so hard all day to live the right way, to suppress the angry retort or the quick sarcastic jibe, that we relax at home and become off-guard. Surely we haven't got to try hard at home too, have we? The only answer to that is yes, but the good news is that Jesus Christ wants to give us a whole new way of looking at our family life; a new heart attitude towards those we love, or have always said we love. When our utopian dreams of romance grow thin, when each day is no longer a 'Valentine's Day', and even Valentine's Day itself is remembered at the last moment with a hastily bought card, we need a fresh motivation!

Selfishness and lack of care (carelessness) go hand in hand. Basically our lack of care springs from that attitude which makes us care firstly for ourselves. Self-preservation is a strong instinct and, unfortunately, many of us as Christians still have that as a primary instinct. As Christians we have an even more basic question to ask ourselves: do I care most for God's things, or mine? If we cared most for God's things then our heart attitude would be right, and the resultant lifestyle selfless, but on closer examination we have to admit that so often we still have an uppermost care for our own things, however deep down it may seem to be buried. Perhaps we often try to care for both, and that is why we find ourselves in the schizoid situation of being one thing at work or church, and another at home.

Paul had the answer right, and could say that he counted all things but loss in view of the surpassing value of knowing Christ Jesus (Phil 3:8). That is why he could then say to the Corinthian Christians, 'I do not seek what is yours, but you' (2 Cor 12:14). The old explanation of the word 'joy' still holds good:

> Jesus first,
> Others next,
> Yourself last.

Returning to our context of family life there is no doubt that we take our nearest and dearest for granted. That is why we need this fresh look at our heart attitude—that we might take a fresh look at our family as people. When we see each person, be they wife or child, in a new way, then we will begin to think innately and more positively about their welfare and about how we care for them. Suddenly we realize afresh just how much we value them, and we are quicker to question ourselves as to how we can make life more comfortable and more enjoyable for them. The hard work seems to be taken out of it. It is now a Spirit-born thing—a joy.

When we have thought through our heart attitudes as a foundation, we can then address ourselves to the practical expression of care at home. The first and most important consideration is that of time—both the quantity and quality of time spent with the family. The all-too-often repeated story of the business 'widow', left on her own for most of the day and quite a chunk of the evening, is parallel to the church 'widow' whose husband spends not only time at work, but also much time in church matters. It may be that his gifts are being greatly appreciated by the leaders and members, but meanwhile his wife and children are growing more and more unhappy and unfulfilled. Why? Because they don't feel cared for. Many sweet-sounding phrases, bunches of flowers, and even the hazardous adventures involved in obtaining a box of Milk Tray, cannot be substitutes for time spent together!

But there is a very real dilemma. Church life is so important, guilt quickly raises its ugly head if people are needed to take up a responsibility at church and we are enjoying ourselves at home. How much time can I spend on other matters before it begins to affect my home life? Wrong question. What should be asked is: how much time shall I spend with my family in order to build a firm foundation? For a long time we have felt church life to be very important for the family, and so it is, but we have forgotten that the converse is even more true—family life is so important for the church! (This we have discussed more fully in chapter 4.)

Family life is the basis for the life of the church. The whole family concept is found in eternity, where three persons coexist in glorious harmony in the Godhead. God's immediate concern after Adam's creation was to find him a companion, and then that they should multiply. God brought not only Noah, but also his family through the flood, and then years later was to tell Abraham that he would be the *father* of a great nation.

Our greatest example was, of course, Jesus. God didn't send him into the world as some kind of adult extraterrestrial being, but put him into a family who would nourish and teach him. His care for his mother's welfare was selflessly displayed from the cross. God cares so much for people to share life together that if there are those isolated from family life he puts them into a family (Ps 68:6).

We mentioned in the first chapter how, for six years, we fulfilled a commission from God to take lonely, broken, confused people into our family home, and to extend to them the love and care which they had missed so much. Many of those people came from situations, where either there were no longer any parents, or where the parents had split up. Family life had been disrupted and the children suffered.

It was not a vague ideal that Paul put forward, as a criterion by which the suitability of a potential elder or deacon should be judged, but sound common sense based on an obvious scriptural principle that such a person must be able to manage his own household well, or how will he take care of the church of God?

Imagine 'Neverchange Gospel Hall', where the deacons run the church affairs and the wives run the deacons! Who has oversight in the church? However gifted and wise the individuals concerned may be, how does that sort of oversight fit in with scriptural guidelines? Now to manage a household well is not just a matter of having every other member of the family under the thumb; having trouble-free financial systems; maintaining a lawn like a bowling-green and a house that makes showhouses look shabby. It is all about having a secure, fulfilled partner, and secure, fulfilled children. If we invest time into our family, not only do we reap a healthy home, but also an abundance of things that will help to build the church. Once we can grasp this principle there need be no guilt if we do not immediately jump to meet all the clamouring demands of a local church.

The amount of time we spend with our family will obviously vary according to our situation. Some will have one child, others more, some will have no children. Some may have large houses, some small. Some may have members of the family who are permanently unwell or are physically handicapped. Some may be the keep healthy, eat bran, grow-your-own vegetables types, who go for regular country constitutional marathons, and who tend a goat, a sheep, a brood of hens and a massive manure heap. There are many factors that would contribute to our deciding how much time should be spent with our families. The one thing we must not lose sight of is the need not just to be around the house, but to actually be with the family. The sort of questions that might prove useful guidelines are: do I know how my wife is feeling? (Happy or unhappy, fulfilled or unfulfilled, secure or frightened?) Am I up to date with my partner's interests? How are my children getting on at school? Have they many friends or are they sometimes lonely? What projects are they involved in and how are they progressing in them? What music do they like and what is their favourite group? What is their favourite TV programme?

If we cannot answer these questions then there is obviously a very serious lack of time spent with the family. Other guidelines would be whether or not there is relaxed time in which we can chat over what may appear to be mundane issues with our partner, or playing games with the children without having to keep looking at the clock. It is sometimes frightening to realize how quickly our children are growing up, and then to realize how little time we have put into their lives, and also how little time we have had to enjoy them. Spending time is showing care.

Perhaps even more important than the quantity, is the quality of time spent. How easy it is to collapse in a chair after work (whether it has been in or out of the home) and to kid ourselves that at least the family is in the same room. The TV is on in one corner, the record-player in another, dolls and Dinky toys litter the floor— everyone seems perfectly happy! But what use is a non-communicative person when the others want someone to talk to, or someone to listen to? And don't assume, because the others don't actually come and say anything to you, that it means they have nothing to say. Maybe they have learned the hard way that fraught fathers and muddled mothers can snap menacingly if approached at the wrong time! Perhaps the family motto is 'Let sleeping dads lie'!

We might even spend many hours at home, but be so taken up with our own thoughts and concerns that in the end it would probably be better if we were not there. It would be less painful for the others. We can judge the quality of our time spent with the family by examining honestly the quality of security and welfare of our partner and children. The guideline for our quality comes from the same root as the heart attitude that was mentioned earlier in this chapter: what can I give of myself to enrich my family? For men it is chiefly to give that which will allow their wives to be released into their ministries; to ensure that they are 'pastored'. For women it is chiefly to give that which will support and encourage their husbands; to ensure that they feel respected. For men and women together it is chiefly to give that which will make their children spiritually, emotionally, and physically stable; to ensure that they can stand on their own two feet.

Having decided what time we need to spend with the family we then know what time we have for other things. When it comes to church life we can serve with a much freer mind if we know the family is secure. Although it may seem at times frustrating to be at home when we could be doing so much in the church, in the long run it is of far greater use to the church to have spent time with the family, because we find that when the family basis is secure, it actually releases us with God's blessing to fulfil a ministry function. We now go out on certain nights, or at weekends, or longer periods if we are in full-time service, representing the whole family—not just as individuals.

The other aim we should have, of course, is to serve in the church in an area that involves the whole family. In these ways we demonstrate our care for our loved ones. The greatest outcome of this is to reveal the caring character of God. We have the ability, through our life with the family, to speak volumes as to the nature of the God that we want our family to love and trust more and more. This is truly caring for God's things.

Many people are anxious to know how I, in my role with British Youth for Christ, can find time to spend with the family. It's very simple really—I can't find time; I make time. The first days to be filled up in a new diary are the regular days and weekends off, free from travelling and other responsibilities. I'm no model father or super-saint; there are times when the children ask Marion when they will see me again, but I have always made a rule that family time is prime time. At the time of writing responsibilities seem greater than ever, and I know that to some extent the family is having to bear the burden, but because Marion and the children have agreed to my fulfilling this call of God, we can talk about it together and have a realistic understanding of this particular period. Some of the current responsibilities involve planning things which will greatly affect the family future. I cannot possibly make decisions on my own within a British Youth For Christ context, or even with Marion alone, but each one of us (yes, our three daughters as well) is involved in an agreement together.

There is another barrier to our spending time with the family, and that stems from pride. There are many who can cope well with daily employment because they are skilled and have authority. Others look up to them and obey their orders and deep relationships don't have to be built. At home it is a different matter—there they find they cannot just issue orders—relationships do have to be built, often through times of personal conflict, and their skills seem to have no particular bearing on home life. Take one of the deacons from the church we mentioned earlier, 'Neverchange Gospel Hall'. At church he is greatly respected for his orderly planning of all practical details. At work he is respected for his great knowledge of computers, and he has authority over many others, who willingly submit to a skill they recognize as greater than theirs. At home, however, all is different—his wife doesn't behave like one of his employees, and neither she nor the children are the slightest bit interested in computers! His qualifications for respect at church and business don't seem to carry the same weight at home. Somehow, although he doesn't like to admit it, it is easier to be at work.

The easy way out of that difficulty is to spend longer at work or, as a Christian, to immerse himself in church activities. Home is difficult, so other avenues are more attractive. Better to be appreciated at church and work, thinks he, than to feel ill at ease at home. This is a way of life that more than a few Christians get involved in. Painful though it may be, the issue must be faced squarely—there must be honest heart-to-heart talking between husband and wife, and then the seeking for power and recognition set aside.

It could well be said by way of summary: take time to care. Caring takes time, but is a wise use of it.

6. Watch Out –
The Women are Coming!

MARION

There is much being said today about woman's role within our society. Women have fought long and hard to have an equal place alongside the men. In their efforts to gain ground they seem to have lost out in the area of their own femininity. It is not a misfortune to be born a woman! If we go back to creation we see that God created woman to be a helper for man (Gen 2:18). We are equal in the sight of God. We are also different yet complementary to man. Paul makes the point that woman is not independent of man, neither is man independent of woman. We need each other.

When we consider the role of woman as a home-maker, meaning one who has a full-time career at home, it is sad that society makes us feel we owe it an apology for being that very thing. Why is it that when asked our occupation we usually reply, 'Oh, I'm *only* a housewife!'? Society degrades our value, but more disturbing is the fact that we degrade ourselves. In reality such a role can be a noble calling.

Baukje Doornenbal and Tjitske Lenstra in their book entitled *Homemaking* (page 4) write:

> A happy homemaker, convinced of her importance as an individual, and as a contributor to the lives of those around her, forms the backbone of the family. And in turn, good families constitute the building blocks of society. Women in the home therefore, can exert a crucial influence on their society.

How can we be convinced of our importance as an individual? Jesus, more than anyone else, cared about women, and revolutionized the Jewish view of women that was prevalent at that time. He talked to women, healed women, encouraged women, forgave women, and taught women. Jesus included them in his teaching illustrations, making it clear that his message involved them. By honouring them in this way he put woman on an equal footing with man, and demanded the same standards and response from both.

Paul also initiated ideas that allowed women to view themselves as equal with men, possessing an identity of their own, and having a right to express their potential in gifts and capabilities.

Because of some negative statements Paul made about women, which are emphasized out of all proportion, we forget it was Paul who said in Galatians 3:28, 'There is neither male nor female; for you are all one in Christ Jesus.' In 1 Peter 3:7 Peter tells the men to give women honour as fellow-heirs of the grace of life. We are heirs of the Father, joint-heirs with the Son (Rom 8:17).

The privilege of being a wife and mother is one which I would never want to alter, but I have found my fulfilment firstly from simply being me. It is very important that we do not look for our fulfilment from a role, but much more from God loving and accepting us for who we are. The children's chorus *If I Were a Butterfly*, has a line which many women would find difficult to accept—'I just thank you Father for making me *me*.'

Let us look at the biblical principles that govern the role of a wife. There is nothing wrong with a wife being submissive to her husband. That is the teaching of Ephesians 5:22. However, the verse before that also asks that we submit to one another. In Ephesians 5:25 husbands are told 'love your wives, just as Christ also loved the church and gave Himself up for her', in order that the church (his bride) might have her every need met, and be complete in every way.

If the husband fulfils his role it is easy for the wife to willingly abandon herself to him, knowing that he is sacrificing himself for her. Too many men still expect submission from their wives, without fulfilling their part. I remember reading Ephesians 5:33b in the Amplified Version, and it revolutionized my whole view of what it means when it says that a wife should respect her husband. The Amplified Version includes a list of English words with the same essential meaning as respect: 'Let the wife see that. . . she notices him, regards him, honours him, prefers him, venerates and esteems him; and that she defers to him, praises him, and loves and admires him exceedingly.'

Our marriage changed dramatically when Rob and I were filled with the Holy Spirit. Rob was no longer trying to impress and be somebody in his own right, and he genuinely began to serve me, and put my needs before his own. This humbled my proud, stubborn nature, and I began to give myself to him in a way that I never had before. Obviously the marriage continues to improve the more we learn to consider the other partner before ourselves.

To become a wife, mother, and homemaker, we choose to lay down our own career aspirations and personal fulfilment in order to serve our husband and children. Husbands too in their way need to make a similar sacrifice. When we give ourselves in this way we begin to have some understanding of what Paul was saying in Philippians 2:5, that we should have the same attitude as Jesus who laid aside his divinity and deliberately chose to become a servant. It is not that we become doormats to be trampled on, but that we choose to serve our family.

It is essential that as husbands and wives fulfilling our roles together, we should seek to work together, to encourage each other, and to release each other into everything that God has in store for us.

My greatest encourager has always been Rob. He has always accepted me, believed in me and urged me on to attempt the impossible. He has spent much time over the years talking and praying with me over areas of difficulty in my life. I have always been absolutely certain that he values me as a person—as someone he can talk to and share his life with—not just his wife, or the mother of his children. Humanly speaking it is he who has helped build my confidence and sense of worth and value as a person.

I am not as good at encouraging him. I try, but I find it difficult not to mention the fact that he did go on too long with his sermon, and he shouldn't have spoken like that to so-and-so. I have to make a deliberate effort to make encouraging remarks. Michael and Stormy Omartian sing a song entitled 'I'm believing for the best in you'. Every wife should learn that line!

The most essential ingredient in our role as wife and mother is that we are secure in our own worth and identity as individuals, and secure within the marriage relationship. We are unique. Only we ourselves can be the wife and mother we were meant to be. Our husbands have chosen to share their lives with us. In Proverbs 12:4 we are told: 'An excellent wife is the crown of her husband.' I want Rob to be proud of me, to be glad that he married me. It is not good for a wife to let her outward appearance deteriorate. It matters how we dress and how we look, even if the real radiance does come from the inside.

As mothers we have a tremendous influence in the shaping of our children's lives. If we do our jobs properly it may be that our children will 'rise up and bless us', as those of the mother in Proverbs 31. Paul reminds Timothy that it was his mother and grandmother who imparted their faith to him and taught him about the Lord. It was the willingness of Mary and her cousin Elizabeth to be used by God that changed the course of history, and made two mothers very special in the eternal story of salvation.

A mother needs to be so many different things to her children. I've listed below just a few from my own experience, bearing in mind that all my children are female.

A comforter: for all ills, for binding up grazed knees, when someone at school is being horrible, when the boyfriend has found another love.

An encourager: to take those first few steps, to make more effort with the homework or music practice, in the first attempts at cookery, in appearance, in relationships with others.

A friend: one who comes alongside and shares in the fun of life.

A wise counsellor: advising on many different topics in the course of a day.

A listener: to all the events of the day, the things that may be worrying, or deep issues needing to be vocalized.

A security or anchor: when everyone else seems to have deserted them.

A corrector: to discipline, help and rebuke if necessary.

The mother in Proverbs 31 also 'stretched out her hand to the poor and needy'. Her care as a mother extended beyond her immediate family. There are many people today desperately needing to experience a mother's love, and the warmth of a real home. The gift of hospitality is one that seemingly few people in the church of this nation have, yet it is needed so much. As mothers at home we can take the initiative to invite others in and show them love.

Mothers in God

In Titus 2:3–5 we have some instructions written particularly to the older women or older mothers.

Paul wants them to set a good example, teaching what is good, and encouraging the younger women to love their husbands and children, to be sensible workers at home, and to be subject to their own husbands. Very sound advice you may say, but where are the older women in the church today? It appears that as soon as the children are deemed to be off their hands most women go back to work. Where work is not absolutely necessary, I would ask them to stop and pray about the possibility of being used within the church to encourage the younger women. Perhaps by visiting and befriending them individually, running a play-group or baby-sitting; somehow investing time in their lives. There are many young women with young families a long way from their family roots who, although they are part of a church, still feel lonely and long for a 'Mum' type person they can turn to for help and advice.

My mother and mother-in-law both died within the space of eighteen months, and through that I lost two older Christian women who had given me unqualified support, encouragement and advice. For some time I felt completely bereft, though through it all I know my relationship with God has deepened. It was indeed a privilege for me to have that kind of support while the children were small. However, as a result of that, I find myself really looking forward to visiting the homes of older Christians where there is a motherly person who cares. We need to realize afresh how vital the role of a mother is, and to see how much we can be used within the church.

As wives and mothers our career as homemakers have a broad perspective. There are so many different

skills involved. We have the ability to make a house into a home. It allows us to develop our own creativity and gifts; it probably causes us to pray for new gifts as well. Just some of the skills we may need are those of cook, educator, nurse, hostess, cleaner, organizer, gardener, mechanic, economist, decorator, dress-maker and electrician. In 1981 'Wages for Women' advocators reckoned we were worth £180 per week. One of the necessities of our career is that we need to become proficient at combining two or three of these skills at the same time. You may need to prepare a meal with a baby tucked under one arm, while answering questions about evolution and who made God to your persistent four year old. I venture to suggest that this is a feat which most men find quite difficult! (The one in our house does anyway.)

The homemaker's role within the church

The fact that women are wives, mothers, and home-makers, does not negate the truth that they are still individuals who make up the body of Christ—his church on earth. What we have to offer to the church is vital at this particular time in history, as the break-down of the family continues to gain momentum. In the church women are needed, who not only fulfil the wifely, motherly role, but who are also sold out to God.

The biggest problem seems to be that male chauvi-nism is still alive and well in the British church, although in the last few years there have been signs of change. If men and women truly have a complemen-tary role we need to see it demonstrated more within

the church. Not every woman is gifted at preparing church teas, doing the flowers, and teaching in the Sunday School! Unfortunately, neither is every man who preaches, teaches and pastors gifted at *those* things!

It is a pity that the Women's Liberation Movement has given the impression that all women are domineering and pushy. As Tony Campolo says in *The Power Delusion* (page 26): 'The answer to 35 million men who are aggressive, pushy and domineering is not to create an opposition of 35 million aggressive, domineering, pushy women.' There is a verse in John 8 that says, 'If therefore the Son shall make you free, you shall be free indeed.' Surely that is the best liberation a woman or man can have.

As men and women within the church we need to work out how we can best be used to release and encourage each other. I don't think women really desire to take over, they have an inbuilt need to be led, but they are looking for men to lead them who have the stamp of God's authority upon them. Sadly, that is why so many Christian wives, who have husbands who are weak leaders, begin to look to another man outside the marriage who has that kind of strength.

It is also worth noting that when women are repressed in a situation they find other ways of having their say. The Brethren Church tried to keep women silent in the meetings, but you could guarantee that they ruled the roost at home, and deacons or elders meetings were often more what the wives had told their husbands to say, than what the men really thought themselves. Rob experienced this as he grew up in that particular denomination, even though he is

very thankful for the tremendous biblical teaching he received.

Some women seem to think that once you have a baby, or a busy routine with young children, you go into cold storage, and you stay there like a caterpillar turning into a chrysalis, until you hopefully emerge again as a real person once the children are off your hands. That is absolute rubbish! God wants to use us to our potential all the time—we can't have any wasted years! As we have seen, there are women who purposely hide behind their husbands and children; children particularly can be used as an excuse to opt out of church life. But God looks on us as individuals, not as someone's wife or someone's mother. Women at home may feel that they have no particular status of their own, but that is where our security in God is so important.

As Ann Warren points out in her book *Today's Christian Woman* (page 105), 'In the early ministry of the church, women were very much involved, and this was all the more remarkable since at that time Jewish women were not even allowed to sit with the men in the body of the synagogue, let alone help or take part in any way.'

All through the Bible we see examples of women in ministry—as prophets, teachers, leaders, deacons, evangelists, pastors, even apostles, if we believe Junias was female (Romans 16:7)! God gives his gifts to us all without discrimination. It is a sad fact that some in the church have been more than happy to allow women to teach and preach on the mission field, or to teach in the Sunday School, while at the same time holding the view that women are more easily

deceived. If that is true, women should be supervised at all times, not let loose on unreached people, and children in their most formative years!

Ian Barclay, Churches Secretary to the Evangelical Alliance, has outlined a ten-point plan to reach the unreached and revive the believers in local church life (*Today* magazine, October 1984). One of his points is this:

> If the clear teaching of Scripture is that the female is a lesser being, then that settles the matter of women in the Church. However, if the Biblical emphasis is different from that, then locally we must start to give a lead in allowing women to find their true place in the Church and the world. Rather than endlessly debating what Scripture appears to prohibit, an area of research that needs to be tackled is the place that women actually enjoyed in the New Testament Church.

Rob and I both believe that men and women have a complementary role. In marriage the wife submits to the headship of her husband, but in the church we submit to one another, recognizing the gifts God has given to others, and those he has given to us. If we keep in mind Christ's words in Luke 9:23, 'If anyone wishes to come after Me, let him deny himself, and take up his cross daily, and follow Me', there should be no question of power seeking, or domination for any individual.

Through our years in Open House, Rob and I have learnt to share our ministry together. I have gained so much from the encouragement of a husband who doesn't see me as a threat, but who longs for me to step into all the good things that God has for me. The role

of wife and mother is one which I find challenging and absorbing, and one which I enjoy immensely, but within that role I have the freedom to be me.

As we travel around the churches in this nation we see so many women who are truly women of God, longing for so much, but who hold back because they are waiting for a man to take the lead. Unfortunately it seems that there are not enough men of calibre in leadership in our churches today. When Youth for Christ launched their Urban Action programme, they appealed for people who were prepared to be 'Godly, go-ahead daredevils', to quote William Booth's words. It is an interesting fact that the majority of people who have responded to that, and who are prepared to work on the streets, and go into front-line situations, are women!

Christine Noble, when praying about the men and women in the church in this nation, saw the women as God's frozen assets—frozen into immobility—and the men as rotting in the sun, not taking up their God-given responsibilities. The first group needs to be thawed, the second group restored! Our prayer is that men and women in the church today will value one another, respect one another, encourage one another, and concentrate on using every individual that makes up the body of Christ to employ the gifts that God has given them, for the growth and glory of his kingdom.

7. There's a Church in My Family

ROB

Reality. All of us long for it—in our relationships with others, and in our own thoughts and actions. Think just how much more our children need reality—they are faced so early today with the seeming realities of this turbulent society; they are much more able to be 'themselves' than we are, because we have learnt to dress up in more and more different costumes to fit the roles we have needed to play.

But we are so often frightened of reality. Real questions that are asked require real answers, but real answers are not always the 'acceptable' ones. So we become yet another individual or couple sucked into the downward spiral of saying what we do not really believe, or have not experienced ourselves. After all, we and our children have to fit into the 'evanjelly mould', don't we?

76

But do we? With that kind of attitude so prevalent, no wonder we are not witnessing the sort of victorious marching-on of the church in this nation, which we all long to see. Perhaps it's time that people started being bold and choosing to obey the reality of Jesus rather than the cosmetic expectations of evangelical Christendom.

All my 'properness' reeled when I asked one of our twins why she wasn't reading her Bible. She was twelve at the time, and this is what she said: 'Well, I know Jesus as a friend; he's living inside me; you don't have to read books about people you know, do you?' What should I say to that? All my pious Christian truisms stuck in my throat when I realized that my daughter had just handed me a piece of reality. The trouble is, it knocked my set pieces from the evangelical rule book for six. Don't get the wrong idea, as a couple we believe firmly in grounding our girls in God's word and we showed her how reading the Bible actually helped to develop her friendship with Jesus. But I had seen that, when faced with unarguable reality, only more reality would mean anything of value.

This sort of thing must force us to rethink the whole gamut of kingdom life in the home, instead of slotting into well-worn pathways that *seem* to lead somewhere, but have actually often been the route to disillusionment for teenagers. We are, after all, stewards of these young lives in order to bring them into the full, rich life of God, not into sterile formalities of godliness that lack power. Once we can throw off the age-old adopted habits, we find it most refreshing to be real. It is quite hard work because we actually have to think

before we speak, rather than rattle off the usual phrases like a salesman in his familiar pitch.

Now where does all this start? It must start between husband and wife. Unreality between mum and dad is not going to be disguised in front of the children. What hypocrisy to encourage and admonish our children to prayer and Bible-reading, worship and corporate time, if we do not set an example. We well know that leaders lead best by example, so why be surprised if we, who may spend little time with God alone, and maybe even less with him together, produce children who are similar? Good friends of ours have been leading seminars entitled, 'How to pray with your partner', and have been amazed that at the seminars the vast majority of Christian men and women present rarely, if ever, pray with their partners. Need we look any further to find the root of our problem with prayerless youngsters?

Mum and dad should be building a prayer/worship nest into which to bring the children, not trying to build it once the youngsters have hatched! Fledglings need the warmth of something already provided, something which draws them in, rather than a structure erected because bird-life says that that is the done thing! Our children should not only be born into our homes and belongings, but also into our prayer and worship together. And that prayer and worship needs to be real. Expressing our real thoughts, feelings, frustrations, joys and sorrows together in a context of prayer and praise is the pearl of Christian marriage. We are not, as couples, merely to be scaled-down versions of many a mid-week prayer meeting, with its shopping list of requests and its note of unbelief. We

are to be the uniting of two people, made in the image of God, longing for him, and believing that nothing is impossible with him.

It's quite embarrassing at first! Usually I would far rather Marion prayed in the same way as I do. I tend to be quite a loud pray-er, with plenty of 'mmm's' and hearty 'Amens', but Marion is quieter and doesn't seem to get as impassioned in prayer as I do. The trouble is, it is often her prayers that get answered first! I've learnt the hard way! Singing together is a vital part of time with God, or at least some form of praise. And, for those who experience such things, praying or singing in tongues together is a great joy. We are even getting round to dancing together, although I have to admit that is easier with the children!

Now imagine that kind of togetherness in God, and introduce children to it. It's real! No set prayers, no formalities, but now a widening of our worship together to include the children. It's so refreshing to have a time where any member of the family can do anything. Obviously, in the earlier years dad or mum will lead, encourage, suggest, but later on the young people will take much more initiative. Often, during these family times, the children will ask quite deep questions. They may have been forming them over weeks, but now there is an atmosphere of freedom in which an honest question can be dropped without creating a hollow thud. Once the family begins talking the answers through, time seems to run out all too quickly, but the children have been left with a sense of satisfied reality, rather than that unsatisfied feeling deep within, which is the result of right-sounding

answers without real meaning.

We need to start with a clean sheet of paper when we think through how to introduce our children to God (or rather, introduce God to our children). It's not enough to just snatch up the latest Bible-reading aids from the local Christian bookshop and, together with a quick prayer for blessings on the family and its pets, hope that the children will imbibe the truth about God, and the relationship that he wants to have with them. It may be that some of the superb material prepared by Scripture Union and others is one of the ways to encourage the children, but only after we have thought through the whole way in which we plan to build them into the faith, and have a clear goal for which to aim. Many roads may take us to our goal, but we need to be pretty specific about which road we are going to start on. We all make mistakes with these things, and obviously there will be times when we need to choose other routes along the way, but the overruling principle must be that we have determined under God the best direction for *our* children.

For instance, it may be better for your children that you sit with them and make Bible stories come to life, or Bible themes to be understandable; for other children it may be better to introduce drama, and let them act out a part of the Scripture; for others it may be more realistic to share a reading together, and then let the children interpret some praise and worship songs in dance. Maybe you will ask them each to pray in turn, having suggested something about which they can pray, or perhaps you will have an open time, and allow them to take the initiative. It may be a mixture of all of these. Our youngest, who is ten years of age as

I write this, still says when I pray with her on my own, 'I don't know what to say.' I stopped making suggestions some years ago, and now I say, 'Well, I'll pray first and by then you'll definitely know what to pray,' and she always prays most meaningful prayers.

Our aim has always been that family worship and local church worship should be as similar as possible. Why should our children have to get used to an unreal church setting, when they should find a glorious coming together of other worshippers who worship in a real way? More about that in the next chapter—much more in fact, because that issue burns strongly within us. We as parents must be longing to teach our children to appreciate God, not to bore them so much that mention of Christianity, church, etc, becomes a tiresome sound to their ears. If our family worship is alive and meaningful, the children will realize its relevance, and not see it as an intrusion into an otherwise fairly realistic life. When our praying and praising together takes into account the problems or difficulties that each member of the family is facing (yes, parents too, without placing anything too heavy on the children) and does not shirk the issue, then it becomes a vital part of the children's lives.

For instance, if a member of our family is unwell, then prayer time would be unreal without gathering around that one and praying for healing. It was on our holiday away this summer that Marion had to call in the local doctor for what were quite worrying symptoms. The girls and I immediately prayed, and waited for the doctor's diagnosis. He seemed to think it was of some importance and arranged for Marion to come to his surgery in two days' time. The girls were very insistent that we should continue to pray for healing, and that evening as we gathered around Marion our daughters prayed some lovely prayers of faith while laying on hands. When she went to the surgery the doctor said that what had been there was now gone, and that, amazingly, she was clear! How thrilled we all were, especially the girls.

We have always tried to show the children that God cares about everything—not only 'spiritual' things, but practical things as well—therefore illness becomes something which we want to encourage the children to turn to God about before anything or anyone else. That is part of the reality of God's care for us, and helps the children's understanding of how fully God is involved in our everyday lives. And, of course, one of the bonuses of that kind of openness together is the ministry which we, as parents, can receive from our children. We're fond of using the words, 'Out of the mouths of babes and sucklings. . .' and very often we use them with a wink or a wry smile, but actually we can learn a lot from the innocent yet real things that our children say. Their uncluttered view of things can provide a refreshing newness to our way of looking at things, and their concern for us as their parents can be quite moving. Children don't seem to bear grudges. Sometimes we have been quite stern with them, perhaps even going over the top, yet they demonstrate their love and care for us the next moment. It is the way they pray for us, or share with us, or the practical way in which they offer to help (it does happen sometimes!) that ministers to us. We miss a lot if we hide behind a parent/child relationship all the time. It is good for us and for them if we expose ourselves to a one-individual-to-another relationship.

If we are really going to take family worship seriously then we need to throw off old inhibitions, and the musty old clothes of convention. We must realize that God gives gifts to children as well as adults, and it is good to encourage the children in the appropriation and use of spiritual gifts. There is no place like home in which to step out in sharing a vision or a word from God, or trying out a new chorus accompanied, if rather raucously at times, by the family orchestra! It is in the family context that children can find that freedom of expression in worship. How good it is for them to be able to express their feelings and emotions before God and the family, rather than to express them in some negative way elsewhere. That's reality! That is what has so often been lacking in the church and in Christian homes. We cheat our children of much of their inheritance in Christ if we do not encourage, and provide for, that openness together. Surely we want our children to enjoy God, in all his greatness of love and richness of blessing, and ours is the responsibility and privilege to open that door and say, in effect, 'Look, this is what God is like—come in and find out!'

Let's pick up on a phrase in that last paragraph, '. . . ours is the responsibility. . . . '. If we, as parents, were to take that seriously, then there is no doubt that most children of Christian homes would grow up with a joy and vitality about their faith. It is so often precisely because parents have abdicated their responsibilities in this most important area that the children's learning of the faith comes more through teaching from others, than through life and example at home. Sunday School, or whatever, becomes the place where our children are taught, and consequently their appreciation of things Christian comes via a somewhat 'second-hand' medium. Many of us would have to be honest and admit that we wouldn't know what to do with our children or, if we did know what to do, wouldn't have the time or patience to do it, if there were no Sunday School. Before you get the wrong idea, I believe that we owe much to Sunday Schools past and present, and there is no doubt that many children from non-Christian homes have come to a real knowledge of Jesus there, as indeed children from Christian homes have grown in their understanding of Christianity.

In the Old Testament fathers are often encouraged to instruct their children. In Deuteronomy 11:19 for instance, they are told to teach the commandments and precepts of the Lord to their sons, not only when they are out for a walk or sitting at home, but also when they are going to bed and getting up! Fairly full-time job, isn't it?! The picture of the Jewish family is a lovely one, with much time spent together in various feasts, and in talking together about God's words and his dealings with the people over the years. It is the sort of situation Christian families should recover today. Television, videos, home computers, varieties of magazines and comics etc, have stolen time from our quality family communication.

I had the privilege of visiting China in the summer of 1984, and during a coach ride we asked our guide what the people did as far as entertainment was concerned. 'There are cinemas,' he said, 'but no televisions or anything like that.' We asked then what the people did in the evenings. 'Oh, they enjoy themselves by visiting one another's homes and talking together,' was his reply. I immediately thought how disadvantaged we were in the western world to have such a plethora of communication-breaking entertainments.

Nowhere is this more true than in the home, where the simple enjoyment of mum and dad sharing Jesus with the children, taking time and trouble to listen to questions and doubts, giving carefully considered, realistic answers, has been outdated by technological ogres dressed in bright, attractive clothing. We talk a lot about being radical, and as we know the word really means 'back to the roots'. How we need to be radical in family life! It doesn't mean being outlandish and purposefully different, it just means getting back to how things ought to be, and doing something about it. It seems easier and quicker to hand the children over to Sunday School teachers, who become a sort of surrogate spiritual parents, and to avoid to some extent our own responsibilities. That can never work properly though. Sunday School, Crusaders, Covenanters, Pathfinders etc, can be ideal for our children as extra grounding, particularly as it is a very necessary thing for young people to have special times of meeting and learning together with their peers. But these things must never be the foundation from which Christian parents build. We ought to be able to say to our children, 'Be imitators of me, just as I also am of Christ' (1 Cor 11:1).

Even if we do take our responsibility as parents seriously in spiritual matters, there can still be a problem as regards how each individual parent sees his or her role. Often, it would appear, mother is the one who, having most contact with the children, has most to do with spiritual matters within the family. On the other hand, because it is recognized as dad's area of authority, he takes on a kind of ministerial role within the home, which can become unbalanced in terms of his other responsibilities within the family. I write as one who experiences problems in the latter category.

The thinking behind all this is very scriptural. We have already seen the verse in Deuteronomy which commands fathers to teach their children. That word 'fathers' is to be taken literally, and is not a word used loosely to mean 'parents'. If you have been involved in counselling, as we have, you will know how many Christians still suffer from a lack of understanding of the Father heart of God, and that usually stems from a lack of a father's presence, affection, or strength of character, during and after childhood. Many Christians struggle to believe that God *really* loves them, and while they can have faith that God will answer their prayers on behalf of others, they seem to have this inner feeling that they don't really deserve anything from God, and therefore find it difficult to receive for themselves. Frequently this is the result of a lack of fatherly love at home. How important it is that fathers demonstrate God's fatherhood! It all seems so logical, doesn't it, to realize that fathers in the home will inevitably shape their children's understanding of God as Father.

I mentioned earlier that one problem can be father's top-heavy ministerial role, but there is no doubt that where dad's influence in the home is a well-balanced one, he does need to take the initiative in spiritual things. Every father has a small expression of church to pastor—his family. He is a pastor to his wife and to his children, and where he takes that role in step with his other responsibilities, he can be that without becoming 'the Reverend Dad'! Fathers cannot flunk their pastoral duties and, one can be sure, there will come a day when it will be for them to answer where their children are in the Lord.

Please don't think that I am making out the mother's role in these things to be of no consequence—I am trying to redress a balance that has been sadly lacking in many Christian homes. There is no doubt that it takes a great deal of time and patience to pastor our children. We can be thankful that we don't have to live with all those whom we pastor! Pastoring our children basically means leading them into the heart of God—listening to their doubts and answering their questions. How frustrating it can be when they just don't seem to get the hang of what we are saying! It's so easy to feel like making some authoritative statement to round off the conversation, when really we have to stay with it, and try to find another way of explaining ourselves. And, as the children grow to teenagers, unless we have established an authority which is loving and not dictatorial, we will find little chance of speaking into their lives in a way that they will take any real notice of.

We are so grateful for the patterns which we, as one set of parents, believe God has given us for bringing up our children, even though we have often ignored those patterns or kept to them so imperfectly. There is no doubt that that has laid a foundation for us addressing ourselves to the problems which we now face as the twins enter their teenage years.

In the end it is up to our children to make their own commitment to the Lord, but never let it be said that our times together at home hindered them reaching that stage or, worse still, put them off altogether. Let home, and mum and dad be the living examples of, and encouragers in, the glorious life of the Lord Jesus Christ!

8. Building an Extension

MARION

'I am a rock, I am an island.' Simon and Garfunkel sang that song about an individual, but it can be typical of the isolation that we experience as a family unit. The saying 'an Englishman's home is his castle' is too often true. We cannot hope to demonstrate the power of God to our nation if we aren't prepared to share our homes. The example of the early church is still relevant today. People around us need to see a lifestyle that is radically different from the affluence, selfishness, greed and materialism that pervades the whole of our society. This chapter is about the benefits—and challenges—brought by extending our home and family life.

In Acts 2 the first saved community of people after Pentecost gathered daily in various homes to break bread, met publicly in the temple, and devoted themselves to the apostles' teaching, fellowship and prayer. They began to sell property and possessions and share with each other as they had need; they didn't own anything but had all things in common. As a consequence of their lifestyle people were added to their number daily. It is significant too that alongside this many miracles were taking place. The Christians were united—they ate meals together and praised together. What a witness!

The word 'community' can cause people problems, as it may conjure up a picture of everyone living together, dressing alike and behaving similarly, with no separate identity or individuality. Most Christian communities are not like that, but it is a very misunderstood concept. In the early church the community comprised the fellowship of believers living in the same locality. In the same way today every local church is a community, and the church universal is one huge community. There is a close link between community and family, and it is necessary to fully grasp and understand the church as a community of people, because it will affect our thinking in relation to the home and family. Howard Snyder in his book *Community of the King* says (page 191),

> The way to work effectively toward the kingdom today is not primarily through emphasizing evangelism or social justice as things in themselves, but through the rediscovery of the church as the community of the King.

When we surrender to the lordship of Christ, he owns us—therefore our houses, possessions, homes and family are his. The early Christians understood what that meant in reality. They gladly shared all things together, knowing that nothing was really theirs anyway. Sometimes our security comes more from our material possessions than from our family relationships. Would we feel secure if we had our family, but no house? Fathers work hard, and mothers too these days, to earn money to make a home. Are we really making a home or are we storing up treasures on earth? To many of us it is so important to own our own house—actually the building society usually owns most of it and we spend twenty years paying them for the privilege! In contrast Jesus' words were: 'Lay up for yourselves treasure in heaven. . . for where your treasure is, there will your heart be also' (Mt 6:20-21).

When we experience being part of the larger family or community of God it is easier to release our grip on those things that we have always kept for ourselves, so that what we have can be of mutual benefit to others. The gift of hospitality in Romans 12:13 is very under-used today. The least we can do is to open our home and invite others in for meals and friendship. There are so many people who would love to be invited to enjoy the fun and fellowship of being in a family atmosphere—those who are lonely, elderly, single-parent families and teenagers, to name but a few. In Romans the emphasis is on hospitality between Christian brothers and sisters, but in Hebrews 13:2 we are also told to show hospitality to strangers. The scope is vast, and it is an exciting prospect to know that in giving hospitality to others we are fulfilling a vital ministry to the church and the world without even having to step outside our front door.

In 1 Peter 4:9 we see that hospitality is not the grudging performance of a duty, but the glad act of a cheerful giver. There are not enough Christians who truly practice the gift of hospitality in this nation. We are put to shame by our Christian brethren in other nations, particularly in the two-thirds world, where there is tremendous hospitality and sacrificial giving from people who would go without themselves in order to meet the needs of others. There is a family that we know in Wolverhampton who truly have the gift of hospitality, and it is a real joy to visit their home. People are made to feel part of the family; there are always others for meals, and visitors staying overnight. Sunday lunch is an open affair and anyone from the church can come. Many people owe a debt of thankfulness and gratitude to that family, who have gladly shared themselves and their home.

When Jesus was speaking about the final judgement, three of the ways he judged the righteous from the unrighteous were in straightforward acts of hospitality—'For I was hungry, and you gave Me *something* to eat; I was thirsty, and you gave Me drink; I was a stranger, and you invited Me in' (Mt 25:35). The emphasis is on doing acts of kindness rather than talking about them. In the words of Eliza from *My Fair Lady:* 'Words, words, words, I'm so sick of words, sing me no more songs, read me no more rhymes, don't waste my time, *show me!*'

There is always the possibility of having an extended family. Today our small nuclear family is usually devoid of grandparents, aunts, uncles and cousins, who were always part of the biblical concept of family. We seem to miss out on much of the closeness and intimacy of the larger family of the past, where different generations lived together and learnt from one another. The elderly in our society have to be tolerated, and there is always the nursing home or geriatric hospital where they can be tucked away. We reckon our modern homes are not big enough for larger families, but then do our children really need a bedroom each and so much space? Rob visited Hong Kong recently and saw how one family were happily living in one room—they never had the luxury of choosing whether they wanted more space! If we view our small family unit as part of the larger community of God we can submit it happily to him and see what he wants to do with us. Art Gish makes the point in his book *Living in Christian Community* (page 85) that 'new forms of family life would emerge if we were to begin with our commitment to God and the church, instead of traditional concepts of the family. This would mean many changes in the nuclear family structure, but a strengthening of family life.'

It is good to know that God's heart, as well as being towards the individual, is also towards the family. He used families and called families to demonstrate his will and purpose throughout the Bible. It was he that created the idea of family when he made Adam and Eve. When he came to earth he put his own Son into an ordinary family. The church today needs a stronger emphasis on the strength and togetherness of the family, because those around us are breaking down and falling apart.

Some Christians like the idea of having an extended family. They rush into it without really considering what is involved, and it ends in hurt on both sides.

There needs to be a very serious and prayerful look at the possible sacrifices and cost to the family, and to the person being invited, so that the position can be viewed in real terms.

The whole family needs to be in agreement, children included, so that the person isn't immediately looked upon as an intruder by the children. The relationships within the family need to be secure. What we are offering to a person moving into our house is simply the joy and security of family life, and if we don't already experience that, it is better not to invite anyone to share it! No family is perfect, or even nearly perfect, so obviously the person moving in needs to understand that they are not going to be part of the 'model Christian family' that never has any problems.

Single people may have strange misconceptions about what a Christian family is like. They may imagine they are going to be cocooned in a spiritual haven of peace and tranquillity. It comes as a rather rude awakening to walk through the door on their first day and be set upon by the 'red indians', who unceremoniously drag them to the floor and sit on them. Children are no respecters of persons, and someone else coming into the family is usually seen as an extra playmate. Our girls weren't quite as aggressive as the 'red indians', but they used to sit on people's laps so that they were unable to move, and make them read books to them over and over again!

There has to be a commitment from the family, and from the person moving in, to accept each other, and to be adaptable and ready to put personal preference to one side, in order to achieve that glorious blend of people and personalities that can be seen in an extended family. When it works well there are so many added bonuses for all the individuals involved. It certainly speeds up God's refining process for us!

When we first had people living with us in our home, we had been married about three years, and we had a nice three-bedroomed house that we took great pride in and kept in good order. The time we came home and found water dripping through the lounge ceiling, where our house guest had let the bath over-flow, was a little upsetting! When one of our female guests decided to burn things from her past which had bad connotations, it was a right move; but did she have to do it in our newly decorated kitchen and melt the new vinolay? For me it was a crisis point again when we had to release *our* house and *our* things to God. Once that possessive attitude has gone it is much easier; all you have to do then is learn to live with people who don't behave the same way as you, and don't seem to fit in with your way of doing things! It is one thing to get married and learn to understand and live with your husband or wife whom you love; it is quite another to have someone else come into your family who you aren't madly in love with, who may have smelly feet, or at the other extreme, seems to have a complete monopoly on the bathroom!

If we are prepared to extend our family, and have one or more people living with us, it is not long before we become aware of the desperate need of so many, who have various kinds of problems basically because they have never experienced a real home, and the love of a family. On one large housing estate in Clapham in London, a church youth worker who is in touch with approximately 100 families, reckons that only two of them have both parents at home! When Jesus preached in the synagogue in Nazareth he quoted from Isaiah 61:'The Spirit of the Lord is upon Me, because He anointed Me to preach the gospel to the poor. He has sent Me to proclaim release to the captives, and recovery of sight to the blind, to set free those who are downtrodden' (Lk 4:18).

Can we do any less? As Christian families we must see that our home is a mission field in itself, a place to gather in those who are looking for a Saviour, as well as a refuge and shelter for those who have been battered and bruised (Ps 68:6). God makes a home for the lonely. Let us follow his example.

The greatest lesson that Rob and I learnt in caring for those people who are disadvantaged and needy came from our daughter, Jo, who was three years old at the time. A young man was brought to us late one evening by some of the young people from our church. We knew him well; he had lived with us from time to time, and we knew that he had a problem with drugs. This particular evening he had taken drugs and then been drinking. The consequences were not very pleasant, and it took four young people to get him out of the car and into our house, as he struggled and shouted profanities. Even then he fell, cutting his head on the pavement. He was laid on our lounge floor where he was promptly sick. Rob had to phone for an ambulance, and then accompany him to hospital, where they pumped his stomach out, and admitted him to one of the wards.

In the midst of all the furore at home, I happened to look upstairs and to my horror saw Jo and Debbie standing at the top of the stairs watching. I was angry and upset that they should have witnessed such an ugly scene. I talked and prayed over them as I put them back to bed, but was very troubled that it would really stay in their memories and frighten them.

Early next morning there was a knock at our door, and the same young man was back, having discharged himself from hospital. He looked a sorry mess as he sat in our lounge, the vomit still clinging to his hair. I was still angry and I could barely bring myself to speak to him. Jo happened to walk downstairs at that moment, and without hesitating she walked straight over to him, climbed on his lap, and ran her fingers through his hair over the cut on his forehead. 'Poor Terry,' she said, 'did you hurt yourself last night—were you crying for your mummy?' She had ignored the outward appearance and behaviour, seeing through to the person that was hurting deep inside, and was responding to that need.

In the years that followed we had to continually try and imitate her simple acceptance of a person. When we moved into Open House, our greatest fear of all our Christian friends was for our children. Looking back we see just how much God's protection was around them, but more than that, he used them equally as much as he used us—if not more. Jo with her pastoral nature—tender-hearted and caring; Debbie with her extrovert, evangelistic, outspoken manner; and Naomi in her own quiet, individual way. Put together, they were a tremendous team. Many times Rob and I, and other workers in the house, would stand back and watch as the children broke down barriers, and spoke to people's lives just at the right time. We had to allow our children to be exposed to situations and people that were not always pleasant or good, but God does not allow his little ones to stumble, and we could recount many incidents where we have seen the hand of God intervene to protect and shelter the children.

Not everyone who has come to live with us has liked children, and we sometimes watched as our children were pushed away or misunderstood. We could not always rush to protect them, and they had to learn at a young age that not everybody in this world would like them. Those of you who are mothers will understand how I felt when I watched Jo, trying to climb on a young man's lap to kiss him goodnight, being physically pushed away. The young man had come to us after contemplating suicide subsequent to his wife leaving him. He had been brought up in children's homes, and he didn't understand what 'family' meant. Jo didn't give up; she persevered, and imagine my joy when I happened to see that one night he actually let her kiss him goodnight, and then sometime later I watched him take her on his lap and kiss her goodnight. What a victory for love! This same man married a lovely Christian girl just recently and in his wedding speech he particularly thanked a little girl called Jo, who had shown him love, and helped him at such a difficult time.

The Bible promises that God is no man's debtor, and that when we give we will also receive. As a family, the benefits and blessings that we have enjoyed through opening our home to others are countless. Many of the people who lived with us are still living locally, and they are like a part of our family, although now they mostly have their own families. Having an extended family is not a one-way ministry. We have received so much love in return, and have often been ministered to by the very people we were trying to help. People talk about families inviting singles into the home as if this would be doing them a huge favour. Actually we as a family have enjoyed getting to know so many different characters, whom we have laughed and cried with, people who have enriched our lives and brought their own aura of God into our home. Husbands and wives cannot hope to meet all each other's needs, and parents cannot meet all their children's needs. Dare to enjoy the privilege of opening your home to others!

9. Parents Rule OK?

MARION

> Train up a child in the way he should go,
> Even when he is old he will not depart from it.
>
> Prov 22:6

It is totally impossible to enjoy a happy family life if one essential ingredient is missing—discipline. If the children are out of control, home becomes a place to dread rather than love, and parents find themselves wanting to do anything to get away from them and enjoy a few hours of sanity elsewhere. Once children have got the upper hand there is no stopping them; they are ruthless in their destruction of anything that attempts to stand in their way. Parents are reduced to a quivering mass, and the door is open to all kinds of problems, like depression or nervous breakdown stemming from a sense of failure and the inability to cope.

Society has a down on authority, and we are made to feel guilty if we smack our children or cause them any unhappiness. It is already being suggested that it could be made illegal for parents to administer corporal punishment to their children, much as it is in Scandinavia. God's views and what he expects of us as parents are totally different. It is quite clear that God holds us accountable for the discipline of our children. The book of Proverbs admonishes us: 'He who spares his rod hates his son, but he who loves him disciplines him diligently' (Prov 13:24). Remember the old priest, Eli? God actually punished him because he failed to discipline his sons (1 Sam 3:14).

Let's never imagine that if we love our children we should not have to deal harshly with them; in fact we have to love our children far more in order to discipline them correctly than to let them do what they like. How good it is to know that when we discipline our children we are obeying God. It is far better to discipline knowing that we are fulfilling a God-given responsibility than to discipline hesitantly or out of our own anger and frustration.

It takes an impossibly self-controlled parent never to allow his personal emotions to be touched, and probably one who is verging on the inhuman, but we can't afford the self-indulgence of letting our anger or frustration motivate or tinge our times of correction. Children respect you far more if you don't scream and shout, and lose your temper—I know from bitter experience! Our children are quick to remind me of the times I have lost control! And don't think for one minute that Rob is perfect! When the children are old enough it is good to explain why they are being disciplined, and to give them the biblical reasons. They will understand and appreciate the fact that God has delegated the responsibility to parents to bring them up in the discipline and instruction of the Lord, and also that as children they must obey their parents and honour their father and mother (Eph 6:1-2). Children have a tremendous sense of fairness and justice, and will not find this logic difficult to accept.

As parents we must take this role very seriously, because our discipline is shaping a generation which, in turn, will shape another. We can all remember thinking we would never do something the way our parents did it with us, and yet almost unconsciously we find ourselves doing exactly the same with our children. Wise discipline is a rich investment.

Rob and I have found it absolutely vital to co-operate together over the way we discipline the girls. The one basic rule is never to disagree over a disciplinary measure in front of the children. If the children find they can play one parent off against the other, it is certain victory for them. You get to know that when one of the children approaches you on your own, and asks you quietly if they can have 50p for something, it could be that they are trying you because Dad has already said no. A common phrase in our house is, 'What did Mum say?' or 'What did Daddy say?' Rob in particular has to stand his ground because the females in our house are particularly adept at playing on their femininity, and adding a large touch of charm and flattery to get their own way (Mother excluded of course)!

Sometimes Rob thinks I am too hard on the children and I think he is too easy-going, and we have to discuss this together and come up with a measure of discipline that we can both agree on. These discussions need to take place when the children are not around, and be surrounded with much prayer. Sometimes we resort to prayer as a last desperate measure when we have a really difficult discipline problem with one of the children, when of course praying is the first thing we should do. We have found it helpful to pray over the children when they are asleep, particularly those causing most trouble! Resist the temptation to lay hands on them too heavily! Parents need to provide each other with a good back-up facility. Perhaps we can begin to imagine how much harder it is for single-parent families where that facility is missing.

When the Roman centurion came to Jesus, asking him to heal his servant, his words were: 'I too am a man under authority.' Parents also need to be under the heavenly line of authority. We can't throw our weight around as parents if we are not prepared to submit to God's line of authority ourselves. Even Jesus said that he only did what he saw his Father doing' (Jn 5:19).

Within the family there is a line of authority which goes this way: God, husband, wife, child—that is God's delegated order. If we move out of our place in line it messes up the whole system. If Mum despises Dad's authority she has no right to expect the children to obey her. In wanting to gain an authority that isn't hers, she forfeits what does belong to her. If Dad abdicates his responsibility, or hasn't got time, he will lose respect and place an unreasonable load on his wife. It is our safeguard that while we are exercising our authority over our children, God is exercising his authority over us. We never stop needing to be disciplined, because God promises to refine us: 'Those whom the Lord loves He disciplines' (Heb 12:6).

One of the twins recently couldn't understand why she found discipline so unpleasant, and we were able to show her that God had already pre-empted her question: 'All discipline for the moment seems not to be joyful, but sorrowful; yet to those who have been trained by it, afterwards it yields the peaceful fruit of righteousness' (Heb 12:11). It is helpful to our children to know that we, as their parents, are still imperfect and need correction. The worst thing we can do is never admit we are wrong, and never say sorry or ask our children's forgiveness for what we have done wrong to them. It is a most moving experience to be on the receiving end of your child's response when they forgive you utterly, completely and instantly, and hold nothing against you—it makes you feel more wretched, but that is probably no bad thing.

We ought to be able to say to our children: 'Be imitators of me, just as I also am of Christ' (1 Cor 11:1). The power of example in us does more to train our children than any other single factor. Children are quick to perceive any hypocrisy. If we want our children to share our faith, any amout of the right techniques of discipline will be to no avail unless we live out what we preach. Surely this alone serves to cast us back on God and ask him to deal with us, and make us those people who are worthy of being parents, and able to demonstrate by our lives what we say with our lips. It matters very much how we go about our daily duties, because our children are watching us, and they know what we are really like. It might be fairly easy to present a nice image to all our friends at church, but our children will always know the truth about us.

Love and discipline are not opposites. They go together, and any discipline must be balanced with constant reassurance of how much we love our children. The two together give them a security which will fit them for whatever they happen to meet in their lifetime. As good, British, Christian parents, we need to be more demonstrative to our children. The sense of touch is very strong, and is very important here. Let's take every opportunity to hug our children, cuddle them, sit them on our laps and kiss them. If they get too big to sit on your lap you could sit on theirs—they may be embarrassed, but they like it really! In all our time in 'Open House' we did a lot of hugging, holding and loving people who had either never known their parents or whose parents had never shown them any physical affection.

In all this, if we are to discipline our children well, the essential ingredient is *time*. If we haven't enough time to spend with our children, we won't have enough time to correct their faults and set them the example they need. Without time we find that discipline is too much like hard work. Who wants to follow through an instruction given to a child when they are having one of those feet-up-have-a-little-rest times? Lack of time brings lack of patience, and lack of patience brings incorrect discipline—or no discipline at all. So beware!

There is obviously much that could be said on this subject, and there are many excellent books written about the mechanics of disciplining children. We have found the James Dobson books and videos very helpful indeed. It is always good to see ways in which we can improve, and to learn from others. There is no doubt that the area of discipline is a priority if your home is to be the joyful, happy haven it should be.

10. Onward Christian Scholars

MARION

'Forward into battle!' Not exactly the first thought that springs to mind as our children, looking angelic in their smart new school clothes, make that first step out of the home cocoon into the big wide world of education! And, indeed, with kindly teachers, play activities, and cosy Christmas concerts, school doesn't seem so bad after all. But unless we understand just what it is that our children are going into, we will find that in a few years we will be caught unawares.

Just like any other system in this world, the education system, unless governed by and impregnated with the life of Jesus, lies in the grip of the evil one, and however well it seems to work out in our particular corner of the country, school becomes the first and major place where our children experience the ferocity of spiritual warfare. The marked lack of real Christian education, the open teaching which often debunks the Bible and the divinity of Jesus, the lack of clear teaching and guidance on moral issues, and the multitude of different values and principles (or lack of them) which have shaped others in the school, all combine to make school an extremely difficult environment for Christian children.

Jesus said to his disciples, 'Behold, I send you out as sheep in the midst of wolves' (Mt 10:16), and that is precisely the setting for our children as they find themselves caught up in the wheels of the educational machinery. The truth, and everything we hold dear as Christians, is being totally undermined. Authority is slipping away. Teachers no longer command respect, and are often unable to maintain any discipline. The very opposite of everything we believe is being taught, undermining our Christian ethics. We must identify the enemy and fight back, so that in our schools particularly we can regain ground that has been lost.

We can praise God for Christian teachers who see their role as salt and light in educational establishments, and for organizations like Scripture Union and Campus Crusade for Christ, who work with schools. The movement of which Rob is currently Director, British Youth for Christ, is sending workers into schools up and down the country every week—and there are tremendous opportunities for sharing Christ in assemblies, RE lessons, lunchtime and off-campus events. But what desert places these workers often find the schools to be! Young people who have little or no knowledge of Jesus often respond as if they have just found an oasis.

The rise in the number of Christian schools is encouraging, because it reveals a growing awareness in the church for the need of holistic Christian education. Not schools where children of Christian parents can huddle together and shelter from chilly educational winds, but schools which open their doors to all, offering a complete education—God's instructions for life in his world. With most schools as they are, however, there is a very real foundation for Christian young folk to be a living expression of the body of Christ in the particular one they attend. If only churches would grasp the importance of the presence of Christian children in local schools. What a readymade harvest field; what a target for prayer support!

Now, all this might sound interesting, but the whole thing comes back to us as parents. If we allow our children to go to school each day and yet never pray for them and cover them, we are indeed guilty of negligence. How dare we expect our children to live by standards totally different from 99% of their friends, and maintain a consistent witness, if we aren't praying continually for them? We have stated in previous chapters that children are very precious to God, and in their simple faith they live very close to him. They are not immune to attacks from the enemy, and when they come home with tales about things other children have said, we need to listen carefully. Not because we are going to rush up to the school and complain, or side with our children, but because often it is a straightforward attack of the enemy. We need to understand that, and be able to explain to our children so that they can be suitably prepared.

When our children come home and ask why so-and-so's mummy encourages them to be aggressive and pushy and stand up for themselves, while we teach that we should love our enemies, they need a decent explanation. Our children have cried many tears and often thought that we were being very unfair because we have not gone up to the school when someone has been unkind to them. We have chosen to pray with them to forgive that person and show them love. Obviously in extreme cases it may be necessary to have a word with the teacher, but taking knocks and abuse is something that is very valuable for our children to learn, because if they are going to stand in this world as Christians they have got to accept that they have to take persecution from others. Children can weather these storms only as long as they are secure at home, and know that we support them, pray for them, and love them exceedingly.

Some children are more sensitive than others, and although we need to nurture that sensitivity because the Lord can use it, yet at the same time we must help them to know how to cope with the pain it brings. The difference in our twins, for example, is quite marked. If Jo was ever told off by her teacher, she would come home sobbing. If Debbie was told off, she would come home and proudly announce that she had been told to stand outside the Headmaster's room.

As the children grow older it gets harder, and they are constantly pulled in many different directions. There needs to be plenty of conversation between parents and children about the temptations and difficulties they encounter at school. As parents we need to back up what we tell the children by telling the teaching staff if we are particularly disturbed about anything—Halloween, the occult, evolution, for instance—three main things often openly taught in school.

What our family is should colour our children's behaviour at school. We should support school events. Naomi worries about Rob going to the school carol service as he sings the carols so lustily that all the other children stare at him, but underneath she is really proud of her dad, and appreciates his support!

When our children come home from school, mothers particularly should be available to them. I have always made a point of giving the time between end of school and bed to the children. There is so much they want to share with me, and they need me to be available. Obviously not all children are the same, but ours talk non-stop, all at once, when they first come home from school, and it's an exhausting experience!

Children talk about many issues with their friends at school, and it is important that they feel free to talk about these things with us as well. Debbie had a discussion with her friends about what would happen if they got pregnant. (One of their year had had an abortion at the age of thirteen.) One girl said she would get an abortion and not dare tell her parents because they would throw her out. Another said her mother would make her have an abortion. Debbie's comment was that she knew we would be angry and upset, but that she would never have an abortion, and that we would still love her and keep her at home. How very important it was that she knew that security would be there!

When it comes to our children's friends, it is important to realize how significant our home is. Can our children bring their friends home and feel relaxed about it? While we don't want our home to become an evangelistic hothouse, we need to realize that it can be a bridge between the non-Christian environment from which many a child comes and that environment which should speak of Christ—his church and values. Our lifestyle is often different from that of many of our children's friends' parents in the locality in which we live. Sometimes our children are embarrassed, but it is more than made up for by the interest that we show in their friends, and the genuine nature of our concern and welcome. It has been a real privilege over recent years to be able to take some of our children's friends to Spring Harvest, and particularly to see two of them become Christians there. What an opportunity we have as Christian parents, to have some influence for God and for good in other children's lives!

Not only that, but we have the opportunity to be an influence in the schools themselves. Obviously there are opportunities for meeting other parents infor-mally, as well as for sitting on boards of governors as parent representatives, and so on. Two friends of ours, as mothers of children in a local school, went to the head teacher and asked if they could start a Christian Union there. He agreed, and on a weekly basis those two mums carried through a superb programme which involved a great deal of participation from the children. Many children attended regularly, and there was very definite fruit from the whole thing. Head teachers are also often open to parents coming into the school to take assemblies, or even RE les-sons—not surprising, seeing that in many schools those two jobs do not usually elicit a waiting list of enthusiastic staff!

The fact that education involves us as families in asking so many questions and facing no shortage of problems, must raise another question, and it is a major one. What emphasis do we place, within the context of our children's lives, on education? It seems as if we as Christians have fallen into the same trap as everyone else—educational achievement dictates our way of life. In fact, achievement in general is seen as the crowning glory of a person's life. People will do anything in order to achieve something—and the quest for academic achievement begins before we are old enough to think it through for ourselves, for it is our parents who often start the process. Certainly God made us to be achievers, but to achieve something for him. Do we place greater emphasis on this kind of achievement than on the worldly kind?

It seems that often Christian parents will do anything to ensure their children get to the best schools, come top of the class, get the best exam results, and then go on to further education. If we were to place as much emphasis on godliness, character development and the like, we could see a whole generation of strong, young Christians producing the kind of leadership which we so lack at the moment. We can be guilty of hassling our children to measure up to our expectations, and there have been many children of Christian parents who, in teenage years or later life, have needed the help and advice of a counsellor to bring them through the problems that have arisen through a deep-seated sense of failure.

Don't let us, as Christian parents, follow the same golden-paved road of high educational standard-setting. It may lead to glory in the world's eyes (though that's not a foregone conclusion these days), but it doesn't lead to God. Our personal prayer for our girls is that he will make them women of God, totally given to him. Yes, of course we want them to do their best and to experience the discipline of learning, but we are not chiefly concerned with how many marks out of a hundred they are awarded by the world, but with hearing God say to them, 'Well done, my good and faithful servant.'

I was travelling with the girls recently on a short taxi ride. As they talked and laughed together, I didn't realize that the window between us and the driver was open. On receiving the fare, as we left the taxi, the driver said, 'May I say that is has been a pleasure to drive you and your children. It is a joy to see children who are polite and well-behaved, yet happy and full of fun. I drive many children in my cab and it's quite obvious that you are a very happy family.' That is one of the greatest compliments we have ever been paid as a family.

Are happy families really that few and far between? It seems like it. Oh how Christian families need to set the example and demonstrate the way it should be!

11. Where Do We Begin?

MARION

Hopefully you haven't started reading the book right here, despite the title of the chapter! If indeed you have read right through, then we are sure that questions must be turning over in your mind and a number of issues are being raised. It is good to think things through in a disciplined way, and to take stock of the situation. Rather than write a lot more sentences for you to have to digest, we thought that we would provide particular suggestions which could act as focal points to aid the reassessment of your family life.

The suggestions for the way forward are set out below in the form of a list so that you can refer to particular ones more easily. Broadly speaking, there are four main areas in which to re-evaluate, namely:
1. Life together as husband and wife.
2. Life together as a family.

3. The family caring and reaching out.
4. The church's work with families and children.

Life together as husband and wife

1. Build a life of prayer together. Don't try and set massive goals which, while they may sound good and spiritual, are realistically unattainable, and will only bring feelings of guilt and condemnation. Agree specific times which you know, generally speaking, you will both be able to keep. If you both come to an agreement, one can then encourage the other if one flags, without seeming to lay on a heavy rebuke or patronizing attitude. Even if you have one time together a week, that is certainly going to bring a new refreshment to your marriage if before you have had no such times.

2. Sort out the priorities of time between home and church. Don't forget, the main question is not, 'Do I spend enough time at church?' It must be, 'Am I spending enough time with my partner and family?' Are we, as a couple, spending quality time together where we really listen to one another?

We have found tremendous benefit as husband and wife from going away for a weekend together on our own without the children. We try and go once a year, but that is not always possible. Hotels do very good Bargain Break offers and, rather than buying that new piece of furniture, why not invest the money in each other and your family's happiness?

It is a time to talk together about the family, your relationship together, to pray about the future and to discuss any major policy decisions. It is so valuable to get away from the situation and get things in perspective. This is where, if no relatives are near at hand, other couples or folk in the church family could look after the children.

Life together as a family

1. Set goals and aims for your family. It's like anything else in life—if you aim at nothing you may just hit something by chance, but if you have an aim, even if you don't get bulls-eye, you usually get very near it. Think and pray about your priority longings for the family. Questions like 'What do we want most for our children?' 'With that in mind, what developments in their lives would we like to see in the next twelve months?' 'How can we, as parents, best help them to attain these things?' 'How can our appreciation of one another as individuals grow?'

Fathers need to ask, 'Am I seeing my wife fulfilled in her life and her walk with God?' 'Does she feel truly released to be the person that God has made her?' 'Am I fulfilling my pastoral role with my children, and leading them into the heart of God?'

Mothers need to ask, 'Does my husband feel that he is respected, and is a person of worth?' 'Am I understanding how my children are feeling?' 'Are there problems which they are experiencing, but are unable to express openly?'

2. Have a clear strategy for discipline. We need to talk together regarding what things in our children's behaviour we will be more strict about, and what things we will not take so much notice of. We must figure out an agreed system of correction, and what punishment to measure out for what misdeed, and so on. Make sure that both parents administer the same correction for the same problem.

3. Plan specific, creative times together. Don't just rely on the fact that, at certain times, you will all be together, but plan for definite times when you will think up some surprises for the children—things which they particularly will appreciate. Not just Sunday afternoon walks and watching TV, but playing favourite games, going out somewhere special, listening to *their* records.

4. Develop a worship life together. It's not enough saying prayers at bedtime and whisking through a quick Bible story; there must be more planning and depth. Really pray and think through what you feel will best communicate with the children, and then make definite times to carry it through.

Allow the children to express themselves in whatever way they want. In fact, encourage them to do so. It will certainly draw you out more, because you may well have to lead them! Use choruses, instruments and dances, as well as prayers and Bible-reading. Encourage the children to set prayer targets and to pray out loud.

5. Allow Mum to go out sometimes! When the children are small it seems as if Mum is always needed at home. Make sure she finds others who will look after the children at least once in the week, so that she can go out to a keep-fit class, swimming, badminton or whatever—something she really enjoys doing. Obviously if it is a night-school class then Dad will much enjoy the privileged opportunity of looking after the children!

The family caring and reaching out

1. Form close links with others in the church. Look out for lonely people, single folk, students and nurses away from home, visitors from overseas, other families who don't seem to mix too well. The popular people are always invited out more, and will probably always invite you back, whereas those people mentioned above will have little chance of inviting you, and probably are seldom invited by others. At the very least our caring can embrace those of 'the household of faith'. It is so good to know that we are the link, for otherwise lonely people, to the caring nature of God.

2. Consider extending your family by inviting someone to live with you. Don't hold back on this, but do make sure that you know God's will in the matter. If only more Christians would open their homes and families, we would see so many needs met and people healed. It's the family more than the house that people need—being made to feel welcome and wanted.

If you extend your family by more than one, or by one who has a real problem, gather a small group of praying people around you who will support you spiritually and practically. The load is so much easier if you know that there are others who will stand with you.

When the guests come to your home to stay, don't be afraid to lay down ground rules and have a certain standard of discipline. Don't forget, they will be part of your family on your terms, not theirs. That is not being unloving, in fact it demonstrates a far greater level of care, because the very thing that these folk are looking for is security.

3. Form links with school and neighbours. It is good to re-evaluate how many links we have with those who do not share our faith. Prayerfully nurture certain links, perhaps through the school, a sports/social club, or particularly with neighbours. Obviously these relationships will develop out of real interest and friendship, and not just with an eye on another potential catch for the congregation!

Prayer triplet schemes have been excellent in encouraging outreach to friends and neighbours. Many have reported exciting news of people coming to the Lord. The idea is simple—three Christians (ones or couples) get together regularly to pray and encourage one another in reaching out to those around. Each one of the three in the group brings three names for whom they want the group to pray. The prayer brings a greater level of faith and, as contacts are developed, things begin to happen!

4. Use your home for fellowship and evangelism. Don't be slow to offer your home for house-group meetings, or any other smaller church functions. Consider inviting a few people round to share an evening, during which you could pray and praise together, maybe praying for the leadership, or the young people.

Have you ever thought of having a coffee-morning, supper-evening, or a testimony-party in your home? It seems quite obvious, but often we think of it as being a major step, and it can be fairly frightening! We know what a good contact point the home is, and there is no doubt that people feel more relaxed there. It means we can nail our colours to the mast quite firmly while sharing in the context of our own home.

The church's work with families and children

We have put a lot of emphasis in this book on the place of children in the church. There seems much that we could say here as regards practical ways forward but, rather than going into another chapter, we have put together twenty questions for you to think through and answer honestly. And don't leave it there, will you? Please try and do something about it!

1. Has your church thought through family and children's work lately?
2. What is the view of the leadership on the place of children?
3. Are the children excited and stimulated by church?
4. When was the last teaching in your church on family life and children?
5. What encouragement does the church give to the development of family life?
6. When was the last time there was a reassessment of Family Services?
7. What emphasis does the church place on children and young people?
8. Are children and young people an integral part of church life?
9. Or are the Sunday School/Youth Group seen as separate to some extent?
10. Do you think the children are being catered for adequately?
11. If there is a large Sunday School, is there a real

concern for the parents of those children?

12. What do you think would be the best way of working with the children?

13. How many people do you know of in the church that have a real burden and gift for working with children?

14. How could the children become part of the regular Sunday worship?

15. How could the children minister to the adults?

16. How could your church rethink the whole place of children in its company?

17. Given a clean sheet of paper, how would you integrate children into the life of your church?

18. How much of this would be possible, given the current situation?

19. What immediate changes could possibly be made?

20. After praying and thinking this through, how would you approach the church leadership?

Hopefully you have thought creatively, not restricting yourself to the usual Sunday School ideas, but opening up the whole possibility of mid-week events.

Let our final note be one of looking ahead—pressing on in order to see our families become living examples of Christ Jesus. We wish you a very Happy Family!

Bibliography

A. Campolo, *The Power Delusion* (Victor Books 1983).

Ann Warren, *Today's Christian Woman* (Kingsway Publications 1984).

Baukje Doornenbal and Tjitske Lemstra, *Homemaking—A Bible Study for Women at Home* (Navpress 1978).

Howard A. Snyder, *The Community of the King* (IVP 1977).

Art Gish, *Living in Christian Community* (Lion Publishing 1979).

Larry Christenson, *The Christian Family* (Kingsway Publications 1981).

James Dobson, *Dare to Discipline* (Kingsway Publications 1971).

God and the Family

by Paul Marston

The family is under attack. More and more people today are questioning the value of traditional family roles and relationships.

This book directly challenges the confused and unhelpful views so popular today, and takes us back to the original patterns for human relationships given in the Bible.

Thought-provoking yet practical, it covers a range of issues, including building a marriage, the different roles of men and women, sexuality, and bringing up children. Paul Marston helps us distinguish between cultural traditions and the Bible's absolute standards so that we can anchor our family living in God's unchanging truth.

k *Kingsway Publications*